A SHORT HISTORY OF THE FRANCISCAN FAMILY

BY
DAMIEN VORREUX, O.F.M.,
and AARON PEMBLETON, O.F.M.

FRANCISCAN HERALD PRESS
1434 WEST 51ST STREET
CHICAGO, ILLINOIS 60609

A SHORT HISTORY OF THE FRANCISCAN FAMILY by Damien
Vorreux, OFM, and Aaron Pembleton, OFM. Translated and
adapted from the original French text, HISTOIRE DE LA FAMILLE
FRANCISCAINE, by Aaron Pembleton, O.F.M. Copyright © 1989,
Franciscan Herald Press, 1434 West 51st Street, Chicago, Illinois
60609. ALL RIGHTS RESERVED.

Library of Congress Cataloging-in-Publication Data

Vorreux, Damien.
    [Histoire de la famille franciscaine. English]
    A short history of the Franciscan family / by Damien
Vorreux and Aaron Pembleton.
    p. cm.
    Translation of: Histoire de la famille franciscaine.
    Includes bibliographical references.
    ISBN 0-8199-0955-6
    1. Franciscans—History. I. Pembleton, Aaron. II. Title.
BX3606.2.V67   1989
271'.3—dc20
                                                89-39609
                                                CIP

MADE IN THE UNITED STATES OF AMERICA

TABLE OF CONTENTS

I.   THE FOUNDER AND HIS PLAN 1

II. FIRST BROTHERS AND FIRST FOUNDATIONS 18

III. THE FOURTEENTH AND FIFTEENTH CENTURIES ... 38

IV. THE SIXTEENTH CENTURY 56

V.   THE SEVENTEENTH CENTURY 71

VI. THE EIGHTEENTH CENTURY 82

VII. THE NINETEENTH CENTURY 90

VIII. THE TWENTIETH CENTURY 98

I.
The Founder and His Plan

So closely does the life of Francis resemble a fairy tale, and the history of his Order an epic poem, that to really tell the story of the Franciscan family there is a strong desire to begin with, "Once upon a time . . ."

It all began one morning in the spring of the year 1208, when Francis was twenty-five years old. He heard the Gospel read, discovered Christ, loved him intensely, and from that point on attempted to place the entire world in a state of praise and all people in a state of fraternity.

Let us follow his journey, which begins in a small cloth shop and ends with the founding of a fraternity with international dimensions. Let us begin by recalling what the feverish century was like that witnessed the birth of such a movement.

A Feverish Century

In terms of economics, the thirteenth century was the golden century. In the West, we see the first great attempts at business. Bartering disappears little by little, commerce is king, the use of money becomes normal, and universal and joint-stock companies make their appearance. Everything becomes an object of trade and commerce. In facing the growth of this new idol, one expects to hear the "Voice" which will proclaim again the necessity of a choice between God and mammon. To make this voice heard is the role and the destiny of Francis.

To this growth of riches there was a parallel social phenomenon, namely, the movement of people to the cities. The new middle-class, the inhabitants of the city, were in possession of both prestige and power, and they made this well known by installing their own urban communes, or governments. As a young man, Francis experienced and knew the excitement of the barricades; he participated in the dismantling of the Rocca Maggiore, the fortified castle above Assisi which was the symbol of outside power. His rich nature, enamored of liberty, benefitted from the destruction of this collective complex which stood as a symbol of servility for the people of Assisi. There existed in Francis an undeniable democratic aspect which helps make him so modern.

Courtesy, chivalry, a pilgrim heart—these are the cultural phenomena which will mark his missionary and itinerant philosophy. He will not hesitate to begin a sermon with a song of knightly love. He sees Lady Poverty as a woman for whom he wears the noble livery of tattered garments. He serves this Lady in the same noble fashion. Surrounded by his first twelve companions, he compares himself to King Arthur and his Knights of the Round Table. His profession into the hands of the pope he sees as a knighting. He envisioned each of his fraternities to be as a "court of love," where the refinements of charity are taught and practiced, and as settings likened to a round table where gallant knights organized their conquests for the kingdom in honor of the Most High God.

In the thirteenth century laymen began to participate in the activities of the Church, if not in its responsibilities. Their role was intensified in both literature and art. They were moreover, associated with works of doctrinal diffusion, and with works of charity. But, sometimes, they also went astray in some of these movements and became anti-ecclesiastical and heretical. Francis appeared at this delicate turning point. His preaching will try to soften, within the Church, the inflexibility of clericalism. At the same time, his influence will protect clericalism from the external dangers confronting it in such lay movements as the Waldensians, the Albigensians, and also the Brothers of the Free Spirit.

The medieval world which welcomed Francis was made up of all these contrasts. On one hand there were disorders, felonies, usury, violence; and on the other hand there was boundless generosity, a searching for God, and a marvelous thrust toward a more authentic love and faith in God. How did Francis of Assisi assimilate and integrate all these tendencies of his own century?

A City and a Man

The childhood of Francis was a happy one lived in the marvelous environment and ambience of one of the most beautiful cities in Umbria—Assisi. He owes his balance of temperament to the realism inherited from his father, Peter Bernardone, a cloth merchant; his gentleness and delicacy to Lady Pica his mother, a French woman, whose example opened his eyes to generosity, which he later called the courtesy of God himself.

In 1200, when Assisi, a city of the Holy Roman Empire, decided to free itself from the yoke of its German occupants, Francis participated with the middle-class and the common people in the assault on the Rocca Maggiore where the imperial garrison was entrenched. In 1202, at the first sound of the trumpet calling for mobilization against the neighboring town of Perugia, he committed himself to defending his town and commune, perhaps to realize his great dream of being knighted on the field of battle. But, overcome in the battle of Ponte San Giovanni on the Tiber River, he was taken prisoner and spent a year in the dungeon at the prison in Perugia. Failure and sickness brought on reflection in the young Francis and led him to the first steps on the path of conversion.

Two years were spent in which sickness, wanderings, repairing buildings, begging, meditation, and caring for lepers were mixed with his generosity. He searched for concreteness.

Then on the morning of February 24, 1208, there came to him a new illumination. On this feast of Saint Matthias, while attending Mass, he heard the priest read the Gospel. "Go," said Christ, "Announce everywhere that the Kingdom of God is at hand. What you have freely received, freely give. Carry neither gold nor silver . . . ."

Francis jumped up. "This is what I am looking for, this is what I seek, this is what I want with all my heart!" He began to carry out the words immediately. He threw down his walking stick, took off his shoes, put aside his cape, replaced his beautiful leather belt with a cord, and went on his way to preach penance and love as the Lord had commanded him.

Several of his friends, curious and inspired by Francis, were attracted to his life and message, but this raised the question of a rule, or a style of life. Now what to do? Together they went to the Church of Saint Nicholas in Assisi where three times they opened the Gospels at random. The first time they came upon these words, "If you wish to be perfect sell what you have and give to the poor." The second time, "Take nothing with you on your journey," and finally, they opened to, "Whosoever wishes to come after me must take up his cross and follow me."

These three quotes formed the original Rule. Francis and his companions then went to Rome to present this primitive Rule to Pope Innocent III; it was approved in 1209. Two other Rules followed thereafter, the Rule of 1221 and the Rule of 1223.

The Rule begins with and in fact is summed up in these words, "The Rule and life of the Friars Minor consists in observing the Holy Gospel."

Rebuild My House!

It is in the poor that Francis, throughout his life, meets Christ. As a young man, one day all engrossed in his father's cloth shop, he brusquely ejects a beggar; but after thinking about it he runs after the beggar and catches up with him in the street, offering him his excuses and then giving the beggar something besides.

Another time, he took off his own clothes and exchanged them with a beggar in front of Saint Peter's Basilica in Rome in order to find out from personal experience what poverty really meant. As a knight, he committed himself to follow Walter of Brienne in order to go and defend the papal territories in Apulia. At Spoleto, he met a poor knight to whom he gave his own beautiful and luxurious knightly equipment. Another experience of conversion led him closer to the Lord.

Another episode occurred around this time (1206) which in Francis' words marked real progress in his conversion. One day, while he was walking in the country he met a leper, condemned to flee from his brothers and sisters and to wander far from the cities. Repressing a feeling of horror, Francis took the leper in his arms and gave him a kiss. Francis' heart, moved to compassion, led him to spend weeks in the hospitals and leprosaria surrounding Assisi, learning of the truly poor. Through these experiences he came to know Christ who had made himself poor for us.

Francis is now the one his own would call, "Il Poverello," The Little Poor One.

It is at this point in Francis' life, in the year 1205 that

God himself intervenes. In the little church of San Damiano, the crucifix above the altar speaks to him, "Francis, go and repair my house which is falling into ruins." Francis takes this command literally, becomes a stone mason, and successively repairs three chapels. It isn't until later in his life that he realizes the true program traced out for him by God; the evangelical restoration of tottering Christianity.

One day, when the brothers were reading the Rule together, they came upon this quotation from Scripture, "Et sint minores!" which means, "Let them be lesser, smaller than the others!" At this time Francis said, "Minors, that is the name that fits us." And the Order of Friars Minor was baptized, for until then, the people had called them, "The Penitents of Assisi."

The Franciscan Charism

What is it that differentiates the Franciscan Order from other orders? Is there a charism that is truly Franciscan? When they tried to place him by force into former traditions, and to assimilate him with his predecessors, Francis replied, "Do not speak to me of Saint Augustine, or of Saint Pachomius, or of Saint Benedict. I am doing what the Lord has revealed to me."

In fact, you can search in vain in his Rule for a complete code of the religious life such as one finds in the Benedictine Rule. There is no mention of monasteries, of horariums or fixed schedules, nor of the method of training postulants. Francis's Rule does speak, of course, as do all the other rules, of the vows of religion and of a daily office, but what distinguishes it from the others is the obligation of poverty *practiced in common* as well as individually. It is a matter of *fraternity* as "sacrament of God," while in Benedictine monasteries it is Father abbot who represents God.

The Franciscan charism is expressed in a number of innovative ways. It is preaching as *"privileged work,"* even if it is done concurrently with secular work. It is peaceful *missions to infidel countries,* which was a great innovation during this period of armed crusades. It is also *submission to Rome* and the obligation of asking Rome for a cardinal protector and corrector in order to be certain of not falling into heresy. Finally, Francis, because he is making his brothers itinerant missionaries, abandons the long office of the monastic orders and adopts the short breviary of the papal chapel. Francis is referring to this short breviary when he says, "Say the office according to the form and the type of the Roman Church."

Throughout the Rule one comes across beautiful sayings like this one, "A mother nourishes and cherishes her son according to the flesh; with how much more affection should not each one love and nourish his brother in the spirit!" And again, "Let the brothers be able to act and speak with their superiors as with their servants; that is what they are supposed to be: the ministers are the servants of all the brothers."

The originality of this Rule caused a sensation among the cardinals when it was submitted for their approval. Having been deceived several times before by various heretical sects, they hesitated. One of them, Cardinal John of Saint Paul, was able to convince them by making this remark, "This Rule simply reproduces the gospel; if we reject it as impossible to live, it is the gospel which we are declaring impractical to live, and that would be blasphemy."

Pope Innocent III approved the first Rule in 1209. According to tradition, Innocent had seen in a dream this poor and miserable beggar holding up the collapsing Lateran cathedral with his shoulders. The Rule of 1221 is an elaboration of the original text. The definitive text, set in a more official format and in ecclesiastical and juridical language, was finally approved on the 29th of November, 1223, and bears that date as its name, The Rule of 1223.

Thus, recapturing the spirit of the twelve apostles and that of the first Christian communities, a common and fraternal life exclusively constructed on the gospel was again at hand. The brothers prayed together, they loved one another, they preached, they gave witness that the kingdom was already among us, and that heaven begins here on earth. Francis would have been among the most astonished if anyone had told him that these actions were implicitly the mystical, apostolic, and eschatological dimensions of his essential intuition and of his foundation. For the moment, he only wished to know Jesus, and him crucified.

The Second Order

The ideal of an evangelical fraternity aroused much enthusiasm, and the desire to imitate it was found among women as well as among men. It was a daughter of Assisi, Clare of Favarone, who was the foundress and the model of the Poor Ladies, better known today under the name of the Poor Clares.

Ever since Francis had renounced his father and all his earthly possessions in the presence of Bishop Guido of Assisi (April 16, 1207) there was constant discussion about him throughout the city. In 1210, Francis preached the Lenten sermons in the church of Saint George. Clare heard him preach, placed herself under his direction, and on Palm Sunday, 1212, after receiving the authorization of Bishop Guido, went to the Portiuncola with her cousin, Pacifica, where they both were invested and made their profession to the Franciscan life. Clare was eighteen years old.

Francis led the two women to the Benedictine convent of San Paolo until sixteen days later, her sister Agnes joined them and Francis took them to the Benedictine Abbey of Sant' Angelo. Here they lived for four months until San Damiano was finally ready to receive these and other young women from some of the most renowned families of the region.

The first foundation was established. Francis drew up a rule for them that Innocent III approved. Innocent IV later gave them the "Privilege of Poverty," a canonical disposition, or right unknown up to that time, stating that the new sisters abandon everything in order to live only on work and alms.

When Clare died on the 11th of August, 1253, numerous monasteries in Europe had been founded after her example at San Damiano. The Prague foundation is among the most renowned.

In France, very early, since the second decade of the thirteenth century, there are recorded foundations in the cities of Paris, Bordeaux, Toulouse, Beziers, and Carcassone.

Two of these French foundations merit special attention. The Order of Poor Ladies was only three years old when the archbishop of Rheims, Alberic de Humbert, met Francis at the Lateran Council in Rome and asked that several of the Poor Ladies of San Damiano be sent to Rheims. Clare appointed Marie de Bray for this foundation; Marie arrived in Rheims in 1220.

When Isabelle of France (daughter of Louis VIII and Blanche of Castile and sister of Saint Louis IX) decided to consecrate herself to God, she had a monastery constructed at Longchamp. Four Poor Clares from Rheims were chosen to form the beginning of that community in 1261. The royal family presided at their installation; and Saint Louis addressed them with an exhortation which, according to the *Chronicles,* moved all present to tears.

The Third Order

Up to the thirteenth century no one had clearly or practically forseen the way or the manner for a Christian to follow the evangelical counsels without leaving the world and retiring to the cloister. The "perfect life" seemed to be inevitably synonymous with the monastic life. With the First Order, Francis had already broken the ancient customs by dispersing his Friars Minor across the world while at the same time safeguarding life in regular fraternities. He undertook an even more audacious initiative in instituting his Penitents of Assisi, his Third Order.

The idea for such a movement had been in the air for some years. A spiritual promotion of the laity was beginning to make its appearance. In 1199 the first canonization of a layman, a cloth merchant, St. Homobonus of Cremona, had taken place, a sure sign of change. Throughout the West, there arose movements of lay penitents, of "conversi." Some of these movements steered toward monasticism and they thus ceased being lay movements. Others such as the Waldensians and the Albigensians mentioned previously, fell into heresy and ceased being Catholic movements. Still others stayed within the fold of the Church, such as the Humiliati of Lombardy.

True, Umbria as well as all of Italy had penitent groups before Francis, but they did not possess the mentality nor the originality which Francis established through his intuition and in his organization. If he borrowed from his predecessors, he still is no less a true founder of his Third Order than he is the founder of the First and Second Orders. This all the friars have read about since his canonization in 1228, in the *First Life* of Celano. This all the friars have sung since 1230 in the office of his feast by Julian of Speyer: *Tres Ordines hic Ordinat* which means, he founded three Orders. Historians know how strong and precise was the meaning the word "ordo" (order) at the time when Francis lived, and he would not have used the term carelessly.

For his lay penitents, Francis used the rule or *Project* of the Humiliati. This *Propositum*, such was the title, is the text that we possess. But especially, Francis gave to his Third Order a long encyclical letter addressed to *All the Faithful.* It is an admirable spiritual directory which expounds on the doctrine and the permanent principles of these pentitents living in the world yet following a specific Franciscan rule of life. Many names through the centuries have been applied to them including the Order of the Brothers and Sisters of Penance, the Franciscan Order of Penance, the Tertiaries, or today the Secular Franciscans.

The Third Order then was at the same time both an active element in the renewal of the Christian life and a vast movement in favor of peace. The morals and customs of Italian cities were deeply influenced by it, and a number of communal insurrections found Christian solutions, thanks to the non-violence of the classes associated with the Third Order.

Who was the first Tertiary couple? Tuscan merchants: Blessed Luchesius of Poggibonsi and his wife Buonadonna. Moved by the preaching of Francis they became as generous to the poor as they had previously been stingy. With several of their friends they formed the first fraternity and promised to obey the rule given to them by Francis. This was in 1221.

Francis, elated with these lay penitents once cried, "I wish to send you all to Paradise!" And by 1226 when he died, the movement of the lay penitents, spread no doubt by the preachers of the First Order, covered Europe with its fraternities. Francis' dream had already found the beginnings of reality in the fraternities of the Third Order.

The Writings of Saint Francis

Francis' spirituality was not only found in his preaching and establishment of orders; he also wrote. Though his writings occupy only a small portion of the spiritual literature of the thirteenth century, scarcely covering two hundred pages, they are of considerable spiritual and literary significance.

Besides the definitive Rule of 1223, which we have already mentioned, Francis' writings consist of: the 1221 redaction of the Rule, less juridical but more spiritual, more dynamic, and with much more feeling; a series of admonitions, spiritual discussions which took place in chapter, a general meeting of the Order, and in smaller fraternal gatherings; a rule for religious life in hermitages; two brief extracts of the Rule written for Saint Clare and her sisters; The Testament of Saint Francis; eight letters of which some are very personal and brief, and other letters, as for example the encyclical letter "To All the Faithful"; and last but certainly not least, blessings, praises, and prayers.

The prayers are of various kinds. They range from a short prayer all the way to the Office of the Passion. He wrote prayers in litanic fashion; the Paraphrase of the Our Father, and finally the renowned *Canticle of Brother Sun,* or *The Canticle of the Creatures,* which is preserved in its original Umbrian text. This poem has literary significance because it is the first piece of Italian literature to be written in the language of the people rather than the language of the Church—Latin. Its inspirational language influenced future great poets, such as Dante Alighieri.

The first contact with these texts presents the reader

with some surprises as well as several problems concerning the manner of composition. With the exception of a few works, the written works of Francis are composed of rather short, and one would be tempted to say, very disparate, pieces. This fact is due not to any lack of inspiration on the part of the author but rather to the method used to compile the collection. The filial piety of those preserving his words did not wish to lose anything of the sermons, the letters, or the prayers of their father. Some of these short fragments, in two or three sentences, condense a spiritual doctrine which is enough to place Francis in the ranks of the greatest mystics.

This man, educated only to the middle-class standards of the day, receives the admiration of many highly learned people. One master who had come to consult Francis says, "My brothers, this man's theology soars aloft on the wings of purity and contemplation, like an eagle in full flight, while our learning crawls along the ground."

After the death of Francis his charism very quickly worked its way even among the intellectual elite of Paris. Three examples, among others, are eloquent testimony of his success: In September of 1228, only six weeks after the canonization of Francis, Phillip, the chancellor of the University of Paris, gave a sermon in honor of the Franciscans who were building a friary at Vauvert, (the site today of the Luxembourg Gardens). He explained to his audience the diverse aspects of Franciscan spirituality and mentioned the marvel of the Stigmata of Saint Francis.

Two years later on October 4, 1230, Guiard de Laon, master of the Faculty of Theology at Paris, gave a panegyric on Saint Francis on his feast day. He applied to Francis the sentence from the Second Epistle of Saint Paul to the Corinthians that he had taken for his theme, "We are made ambassadors for Christ."

On July 13, 1231, it is a textual citation from Admoni-

tion VI of Saint Francis which is used and expressly com-
mented on by another Master of the University—this time a
Dominican. After a discussion of certain preachers "who
talk and do not act," who are "daring hypocrites when it is a
matter of echoing the word of the Lord, but who reveal
themselves as empty and lazy when it comes to the moment
of action," the orator exalts the simple and the unlearned
who have become saints because they act in knowing the
"fullness of the law, which is love." And it is here he intro-
duces the citation from the text of Saint Francis, "Therefore,
it is a great shame for us, servants of God, that while the
saints actually did these things, we wish to receive glory and
honor by merely recounting their deeds."

Franciscan Spirituality

What then is the fundamental intuition of the spirituality of Saint Francis? To admire, to accept, and to bring about
the plan of God—this is the spirituality of the true Christian.
But what gives to each of his religious attitudes, to each of
his reflexes, to each of his words its peculiar coloration is
the intensity of his love for Jesus Christ.

His love for Jesus Christ! The entire spiritual universe
of Francis rests on the personal and living experience of
Jesus Christ. His religion is not an intellectual system built
upon abstract idea; it is a personal relationship with the one
who explains everything and receives everything, Jesus the
Christ. In Jesus, Francis discovers at the same time the
sublimity of God, his transcendence, and also what he calls
the "humility" of God, his immanence. These two aspects,
far from weakening, strengthen and reinforce each other.

Both of these aspects are fundamentally inseparable.
In the mystery of the Word Incarnate through love, Francis
grasped the continual coming and going, a back and forth

between the two extremes. He grasped both of them at the same time, seeing that the bond between the two extremes, that which filled up everything in between, was love.

"The Lord of Glory!" How many times in his prayers did he thus address the Most High. He prayed to him in long and ardent litanies, composed either of superlatives (all Good, all Sweet, etc.), leaving the world in order to bask in the perfection of God; or composed of negatives (invisible, ineffable, unutterable, impenetrable) leaving creation in order to adore the one who is wholly Other. But, and this is the paradox, he cries out in another formula which reveals his refined exaggeration if it were not dictated by his astonishment in the face of this mystery. "O sublime humility, O humble sublimity!" In the eyes of Saint Francis the most beautiful light projected upon the greatness of God is the visible expression which God gives of himself through humbling himself. It is the approach by which he makes himself, through his humanity, the savior, the brother, and the servant. To demonstrate these prayers, here are examples from among two of the shortest, and ones which we know best.

The first he recited before the Crucifix of San Damiano at the beginning of his conversion, when he was still finding his way. You will notice in this beginner a profoundly God-centered attitude, and a ready openness to all generosity.

"Most High, Glorious God, enlighten the darkness of my heart and give me, Lord, a correct faith, a certain hope, and a perfect charity, sense, and knowledge, so that I may carry out your holy and true command. Amen."

As for the second, it is a prayer which ends a letter that Francis addressed one day in 1226, at the end of his life, to his brothers reunited in chapter. It is of such density and cohesion as to discourage translation. It provides a beautiful proof of the influence of liturgical texts on the piety of the Poverello. It sums up almost the whole of the Christian life: at the beginning, the nothingness of man; but at the end, union with God; in between the grace and the imitation of Christ.

"Almighty, eternal, just, and merciful God, grant us in our misery the grace to do for you alone what we know you want us to do, and always to desire what pleases you. Thus, inwardly cleansed, interiorly enlightened, and inflamed by the fire of the Holy Spirit, may we be able to follow in the footsteps of your beloved Son, our Lord Jesus Christ. And by your grace alone, may we make our way to you, Most High."

For Francis, Christ is at one and the same time the human Jesus and the Lord of Glory, the mediator of being, of knowledge, and of life. Such is the person Francis loves and the one he wishes to imitate and become like. This vision of faith which explains his attitude toward God also explains his attitude toward all of creation—he cannot see Christ without thinking of God and he cannot see any creature without thinking of our common Father.

This explains his sense of fraternity, and why he considers himself a brother toward every person and also toward every creature, toward every being whoever it may be, especially the most humble since it is in making himself humble that God revealed himself so great and loving. Brother Sun, Sister Moon, Brother Fire, Sister Water, these are not hollow cliches on his lips or formulas of poetic license. For Francis, these expressions are charged with a profound religious sense. In each creature he contemplates and sees the touch of the Most High who has created it. And thus he understands the role of each person in relation to creation, not to dominate it nor to enslave it, but to construct and bring to perfection the universe in the way that

God wished. All of this is done in the service of creatures, to orient and turn the person back to God. In short, to preach the gospel to every living thing.

His spirituality is that of a "son of the King." He knows that nothing belongs to him, but at the same time he possesses everything because his father loves him, and as an astonished child, he is conscious of having received everything and he places all his happiness in recognizing, distributing, and handing back everything that he has received. To love, for him, consists in giving everything back to his Father.

Such was the secret of the remarkable flowering of the gospel in the thirteenth century. The Spirit of God, directing the history of the Church, inspired the contemporary popes to have the wisdom and the courage to welcome the reforming initiative of this man in rags, despite the disturbing resemblances to the heretical movements of the day. Francis realized this remarkable feat of being the most free person in the Church and at the same time the most docile to the hierarchy. Having experienced the freedom of the children of God of which St. Paul speaks, he leaps with joy beyond formalistic religion without ceasing, nevertheless, to be affectionately submissive to the one he called Mother, the Church.

Freedom and docility, contrasting yet complementary, will be found all along the seven centuries of the history of the Order. This will sometimes bring about sorrowful tensions, but more often remarkable progress. Let us page, then, through the bright and dark pages of this history of the Franciscan movement.

II.
First Brothers and
First Foundations

Statistics and Geography

Even before the death of Saint Francis, his Order had been spreading throughout Europe. Around 1220, it already counted five thousand religious and a century later, in 1340, there were 1,435 friaries and thirty to forty thousand religious.

Primarily, what characterized the great thrust of the Friars Minor of the thirteenth century is the urban spread of friars. To be sure, the monasteries of the older orders were not all founded in solitude, but as a general rule the monks retired from the world, having constructed their abbeys outside the cities, in the open fields or the forests or on mountains. The Franciscans and Dominicans, sent into the world, not withdrawing from it, opted for the cities.

To three Franciscan chroniclers, who were both witnesses and actors, special thanks are due to their attentive eye and sprightly pen which helps us relive the wanderings and the foundations in the different countries of Europe. To these, history extends its gratitude: Jordan of Giano for Germany, Thomas of Eccleston for England, and Salimbene for Italy and France.

Jordan of Giano tells us that in 1217, the general chapter sent sixty friars to Germany and to Hungary. Alas!

Reduced to begging, being lay preachers, and suspected of heresy, they were taken for heretics and accorded all kinds of insults and bad treatment. Four years later, a second expedition had more success. First, they were led by a native of the area, Caesar of Speyer. Secondly, there were only twenty-seven religious. But, arriving in Bavaria, "the little band...now counted thirty-one religious." At Augsburg, the bishop received them with open arms and his nephew gave them his own house. From there they spread into other surrounding areas, some towards Salzburg, others toward Ratisbonne, even others, in larger numbers, spread out to Mainz, Speyer, and Cologne.

These beginnings of Franciscan history in Germany have all the aspects of the Fioretti. In the words of Jordan of Giano, "At the general chapter of 1221, Saint Francis was very weak and sat at the feet of Brother Elias. Everything that had to be said at the chapter on the part of Saint Francis was spoken by Brother Elias. Saint Francis pulled on his tunic, Brother Elias bent over and listened, then straightened up and said, 'Brothers, The Brother says this (meaning Blessed Francis, who was thus called by the other brothers 'The Brother,' he being the Brother par excellence). There is a certain region called Germany, where pious Christians live. You have often seen them travelling through our country with their long staffs and wearing large boots. They sing the praises of God and the saints as they travel. Covered with sweat, braving the heat of the sun, they go to visit the tombs of the apostles. And because once the brothers who went among them were maltreated, The Brother does not force anyone to go there. But if there are some who desire to go there, let them arise and may they gather here on one side!' Inflamed by the desire of martyrdom, nearly ninety friars arose, offered themselves to death, and came and gathered as they had been ordered . . .

"Their head was Cesar of Speyer, who chose the friars who would go with him. He chose John of Pian Carpino, who preached in Latin and in Lombard; a German, Friar Barnabas; Friar Thomas of Celano, who wrote the *First Life of Saint Francis;* Joseph of Treviso; Friar Abraham, a Hungarian; another German cleric, Conrad; a priest, Peter of Camerino; and a deacon, Jordan of Giano . . .

"In 1224, this same Brother Jordan and the brothers of Mainz, took the road for Thuringia and came to Erfurt on the feast of St. Martin, November 11. As it was winter, it was not the time to build. On the advice of the inhabitants of the city and several members of the clergy, the brothers installed themselves outside the walls, at the house of the priest in charge of the lepers . . . . The following year, on the advice of the parish priest, and of other citizens of Erfurt, the brothers moved to the Church of the Holy Spirit. Here they remained for six full years. The man who was appointed by the brothers to be the procurator for them asked Brother Jordan if he wished to have a house built after the fashion of a cloister. But he who had never seen a cloister in the Order, replied, 'I do not know what a cloister is, just build us a house near the water so that we can go down and wash our feet.' And this was done."

The first friary in France, founded in 1217, was built on the side of the hill of Vezelay, a city of considerable importance at that time. The friary was named La Cordelle, and its inhabitants "les cordeliers," the cordbearers, because of the cord which every Franciscan wore. Two years later, in 1219, a friary was begun at Paris, or more exactly, at Saint Denis. This friary housed thirty religious. In 1234, King Louis ix built a friary for these men with a fine paid by Enguerrand de Coucy. One by one, other cities like Rouen, Senlis, Abbeville acquired these new preachers of the gospel. All the great cities of Belgium had their friaries. In 1260 there were already thirty-six friaries there.

It was the friars from France who established the Order in England. Their mission or departure was not decided at the chapter in 1217 as had been done for Germany and the Holy Land, but in 1223. Let us look at a few sections from the Chronicle of Thomas of Eccleston.

"Under the direction of Agnellus of Pisa, nine friars, among whom there were three Englishmen and a Frenchman, left Fécamp on a boat provided for them by the Benedictines of that city and landed at Dover September 10, 1224. They reached Canterbury where four of them stayed with Agnellus while the other five continued on to London. From there two friars went on to Oxford which became the principal residence of the Friars Minor in England. The foundation of Northampton followed almost immediately. Before 1230, the friars had friaries in Norwich, Cambridge, Lincoln, Nottingham, Leicester, and Glouchester. Thirty-two years after their arrival in Great Britain, the friars had forty-nine friaries, without counting those of Ireland and Scotland where they had arrived around 1232.

"The first five friars of Canterbury had the joy of living in a small room on the first floor of a schoolhouse where they remained constantly shut in day after day. But when the students returned home in the evening, they went into the schoolhouse where they sat and built a fire for themselves. They sat next to the fire and sometimes, when they had to have their collation, they put on the fire a little pot containing the dregs of beer, and they dipped a cup into the pot and each drank in turn and each one would speak some words of edification.

"The first novice received was a young man of good disposition and elegant appearance, Brother Solomon. Named procurator of the friary, he would go to the door of his sister to beg alms. But she, when she brought him some bread, turned her face away, saying, 'May the hour be cursed in which I ever saw you!' But he received the bread with joy and departed . . .

"The brothers would sing the office with such fervor that, more than once, matins lasted all night.

"The brothers were at all times so joyous and happy amongst themselves that they could hardly keep from laughing when they saw one another. Wherefore, since the young brothers of Oxford were all too frequently given to laughter, it was enjoined upon one of them that he would receive the discipline as many times as he would laugh in choir or at table. It happened, however, that after he had received the discipline eleven times in one day, he still could not restrain himself from laughing. That night, he saw in a dream the whole friary gathered in the choir and the brothers were tempted to laugh as usual, and behold the crucifix that was standing at the entrance to the choir turned toward them as though alive and said, 'They are the sons of Core who laugh and sleep in the hour of the cross!' (allusion to the Book of Numbers, Chapter XVI.) The Crucified tried to free his hands from the cross as though wishing to descend and to depart. The guardian of the friary immediately went up and fixed the nails in such a way that He could not descend. The novice told about this vision. The friars were terrified. From that time on, they abstained from laughter, at least in an excessive fashion . . .

"However, one day one of the friars was in a melancholic humor and Brother Peter made him drink a cup full of the best wine as a penance. The brother drank against his wishes as Brother Peter told him, 'Ah, most dear brother, if you would often practice a similar penance, I think you would really have a better conscience!'"

Structures, Mobility, Adaptations

Besides the establishment of their friaries in urban areas, another characteristic of the friars is their extreme mobility. The monks took vows of stability and remained in one place in order to meet and know God in contemplation. Franciscans almost made itinerancy a virtue, in order to meet God in people everywhere, since one of their objectives is to preach to every creature that the kingdom of God is at hand.

During this time, anyone who took to the road was assured of meeting examples of this new group of penitents, who went from city-to-city and mingled with the crowds. Since everyone walked along the same roads, lengthy conversations took place along the way. There was as much good done along the road as in the most illustrious pulpits. This phenomenon of wandering religious, the leaven which makes the bread rise, is something unique in the history of the Church. The canons and prescriptions of the great Fourth Lateran Council of 1215 would have become dead letters if they had not found these mobile units of Christianity. All along the pilgrim roads of Puy, Compostella, or of Jerusalem, friars brought these letters to life and helped them penetrate the hearts of men and women, as they spoke gently of the Child in the Crib, of Jesus Crucified, his Mother, and of the lord pope.

Because of the numerical and geographical extension of the Order, it was necessary for the friars to bring some changes and adaptations to their Rule. They were very careful that the spirit of the Rule was preserved safe and secure, despite the changes in details. Three examples will suffice and are enlightening; trips on horseback, the handling of money, and the building of friaries in stone.

Trips on horseback had been forbidden, since horses were owned solely by the rich. But it was necessary to bring about adaptation to circumstances, especially the necessities of the apostolate. On the 30th of April, 1250, Pope Innocent IV dispensed the friars on mission from the paragraph of the Rule forbidding horseback riding.

A more serious concession, on the 17th of March, 1225, during Francis' lifetime, was a papal bull dispensing the friars in Morocco from the interdict against touching money.

The building of friaries also had to undergo a change. The huts of Rivo Torto were a thing of the past. The time had also passed when Jordan of Giano, while establishing the friars at Erfurt, responded to the city fathers who had offered to build them a cloister, "In our Order, we do not know what that is."

Saint Bonaventure himself explains in 1250 why the friars were living in great cities and large friaries. "It is first and foremost," he said, "in order to be at the service of those who require our ministry." And then because, "a better discipline and the fact we can celebrate the office with more dignity and solemnity is why the friars live in large friaries." And to that he added the presence of economic reasons: "In the cities, land is more expensive than in the country; and since it is not possible to acquire the same amount of land, we are obliged to build friaries higher than several floors. On the other hand, in the cities, fires break out more frequently which spreads from house-to-house, and we are then forced by this to build our friaries in stone in order to preserve our friaries, our churches, and our books. These stone walls reassure our poor sick brethren, and even the neighbors themselves, and also spare new expenses of reconstruction which always fall on our poor benefactors."

In the course of seven centuries, the three Franciscan Orders have built thousands of churches and religious houses. Always remaining alive, despite all the reasons of health, studies, economy, prayer, or efficiency, a nostalgic and romantic sentiment for the early days is found in the heart of the author of the *Sacrum Commercium*. Listen, as he imagines Lady Poverty visiting earth, and being received among the friars. "These say to her, 'Let us begin by refreshing ourselves, if you so desire.'"

"'Beautiful idea,' says Lady Poverty. 'But first, bring some water and a towel in order to wash ourselves.'"

"They hurried around and then presented to Lady Poverty a half-vase of terracotta. They did not have an entire vase in the friary which they were able to fill with water. Then, pouring the water on her hands they looked around here and there in search of a towel. Not finding one, one of the brothers held out his tunic to her . . .

"Then they led her to a place to eat. Lady Poverty looked around and saw only three or four pieces of barley bread resting on a little pile of herbs . . . a single bowl . . . no fork, no wine.

"Then she asked them to show her the cloister. They led her up a hill and had her admire the splendid panorama. 'My Lady,' they said, 'there is our cloister!'"

Mission Activity

Religious life is one of the forms of witness to the faith. "Italy," writes Paul Sabatier, "can be thankful because of Saint Francis and his sons and daughters. Infested as was Languedoc in France with Catharism, Italy was purified of Catharism by Saint Francis. Before the eyes of his contemporaries a new ideal suddenly burst forth, before which all these bizarre sects disappeared, as birds of the night flee before the first rays of the sun."

As well as witnessing to the faith, religious life is a means of winning souls. Let us look at the missionary activity of the Order.

Starting in 1219, Friar Berard and his four companions preached the gospel among the Moors of the kingdom of Granada, and had gone on to Marrakesh, where they suffered martyrdom in 1221. On hearing the news, Francis exclaimed, "Finally I can say that I have five real Friars

Minor!" In 1227, Friar Daniel and his companions were martyred at Ceuta. Other friars had gone as far as Tunisia by 1226, and there they maintained themselves rather courageously until by 1270 they had obtained the liberty to preach.

In the Near East, the Franciscans have played and still play an important missionary role. The Province of the Holy Land had already been founded at the first general chapter of the Order which was held on Pentecost, the 14th of May, 1217. At this chapter the world was divided into twelve provinces and these territories were divided among the friars. The group intended for the East left immediately, having as its leader the renowned Brother Elias. In 1263, there were twenty-two friaries in the Holy Land and six monasteries of Poor Clares.

On the beginnings of the Order in the Holy Land, we have one of the finest witnesses, that of the bishop of Saint Jean of Acre, Cardinal Jacques de Vitry. An eyewitness of the siege of Damascus, Jacques de Vitry confirms firsthand the account of the biographer of Saint Francis on his trip into Egypt and on his participation in the fifth crusade. Here is his account.

> We have seen the founder of this Order, a simple and unlettered man, loved by God and all people; he is called Brother Francis. Arriving at the camp of the Christians before Damietta, without any fear, and fortified only by his faith, here he is leaving for the camp of the Sultan of Egypt. The Saracens stop him along the way. "I am a Christian," he says, "take me to your master." They lead him away. At the sight of the man of God, the Sultan, this cruel beast, becomes all gentleness and kept Francis with him for several days and listened to him with much enthusiasm and attention as he preached to him and to his people the faith of Christ. But finally he was afraid of seeing

many of his men go over to the Christian army through the efficacious words of this man who would have converted them to Christ. He had Francis conducted to our camp with many marks of honor and signs of security, not without having said to him, pray for me, that God may deign to reveal to me the law and the faith that pleases him more."

In 1227, Pope Gregory IX announced a new crusade. He sent preachers into all the cities of Europe in order to raise an army. And here is how one of them, a Franciscan, William de la Cordelle, undertook his task one day. He found a place for himself to preach. The knights did not want to run the risk of being won over, and forbade him to preach. "Allow me only," he said, "to say several words, without preaching a sermon." They consented. Climbing up on a wagon, Brother William cried out, "Count so-and-so here, does he have any knights?" Several knights presented themselves as being in the service of the count. Then he asked about a second count, and a third, and a fourth, always asking if they had any knights present. And the men of arms came running proclaiming that they were in the service of this or that count. Everyone kept silent. Brother William then began to weep and lament, tearing out his hair, "Curses on me. All the barons and counts have their knights, and Christ Our Lord has none." Deeply touched, one of the more renowned lords came to the assistance of Brother William and received the cross. After him, everyone received the crusader's cross.

The cities, and thus the friaries and the parishes of the Holy Land, knew many ups and downs during the course of the thirteenth century. Jerusalem, in particular, recovered from the Moslems in 1229, was lost again in November of 1239. The French retook it in 1240, being able to retain it for only four years. The last hope of reconquest vanished in 1291 with the fall of Acre. The friars were forced to undergo the repercussions of this change of the fortune of arms. Many were martyred during this time. The number of Franciscans martyred in the seven centuries during their ministry in the Holy Land is more than four thousand! The last six were martyred in 1920.

After the Near East, the Far East also became a field of missionary endeavor for the friars. In the middle of the thirteenth century, when the Mongol invasion swallowed up Russia and threatened Hungary and Saxony, the friars wanted to see a new field of activity opened to their work. In 1245, Friar John of Pian Carpino was nominated by Innocent IV as ambassador to the Great Khan of the Tartars. At the age of sixty-three, Friar John undertook, on foot, the trip across Lithuania, through the Urals, through Turkey to Manchuria; and the first mission to China among the Golden Horde was begun by the poor friars. In 1251, Brother William of Rubruck took his turn. In 1289, John of Montecorvino himself, charged with a mission to the Great Khan by Nicholas IV, chose to go through Armenia, Persia, and India. At Pekin, where he was archbishop, he built a cathedral, a friary, and a seminary. He consecrated seven Franciscans as bishops to have them as his assistants. All these pioneers prolonged the effect of their teaching through the translation of the Gospels, by a daring adaptation for the time—celebrating Mass in Chinese, and by attempts at a popular Christian painting reflective of Chinese culture. The accounts of their trips, which we still possess, give ample testimony to their remarkable qualities of psychological observation as well as their missionary fervor.

Life in the Friaries

One of the strengths of the Order in the thirteenth century, one of the secrets of its dynamism, is the admirable

diversity which was prevalent as much in individual vocations as in the orientation of life in fraternity. Respect for
personal charism, a democratic tendency, the tolerance
with respect to individual initiatives, favored the openness
to a wide range of possibilities. Even while living the same
ideals, fraternities might be different.

This certainly did not take place without risks. Even
from its beginnings, the Order experienced a certain tension
between rigorists and moderates. On the question of poverty especially, scurrilous satires were exchanged among
various factions. A narrow sectarianism was part of this.
Under the pretext that Francis, besides drawing up the Rule,
had also written a rule for brothers in hermitage and also a
Testament to which some attributed the force of law, the
extremists, or Spirituals, insisted on the contemplative life
to combat those who desired to promote studies or the
active life, and who, although living in large friaries with
sixty to one hundred confreres, did not believe themselves
less faithful to the Rule and their vocation. It was the eternal
conflict between the prophet and the priest, between mission and institution. The repercussions were felt in several
areas; with the help of common sense, and also the gentle
firmness of Saint Bonaventure, the minister general of the
Order, the first crisis was overcome, and peace was re-
stored.

The unity of the Order was based on several grand
principles: fraternal love between priests and non-priests,
between superiors and subjects, each participating according to his calling for the common good of all. One characteristic example is that when the envoys of the pope brought
the cardinal's hat for the minister general, Saint Bonaventure, he was in the process of washing dishes.

Another important factor of unity was the annual
general chapter. Foreseen in the Rule, it was concretely
realized as a joyful reunion, as a session of studies where

experiences could be shared and new orientations looked forward to, and finally as an internal juridical restatement for the improvement of the structure and the Constitutions of the Order. Here is the testimony of an eyewitness, Jacques de Vitry, bishop of Acre, in a letter of 1216. "Once a year, the men of this Order meet at a convenient place, in order to rejoice in one Lord and eat together; and there is a great profit for all. They seek the counsel of upright and virtuous men; they draw up and promulgate holy laws and submit them for approval to the Holy Father, then they disband again for a year and go about through Lombardy, Tuscany, Apulia, and Sicily."

Another element of unity was the liturgy. During this time, each diocese had its own liturgy, a serious inconvenience for those who travelled and had to adapt themselves to a variety of rituals, lectionaries, and calendars. The Friars Minor adopted once and for all the liturgy of the Roman curia, which brought about a unity of ceremonies and liturgical books in the whole Order. Even in the area of plainchant, a Franciscan school was born, whose first great composer was Julian of Speyer, master of the chapel of Saint Louis the King. This Franciscan school was characterized by bold and joyful melodies, which often borrowed from the repertoire of the troubadours. It became less intellectual and more lyrical, stirring up sentiment expressed in short popular melodies; one finds here a trait of a completely authentic Franciscan art form.

Uniformity in the Order was also brought about by the unity of action, by the custom of the same tasks accomplished according to the same methods and with the same spirit. Brothers of various countries felt closer to each other, particularly because in every friary there was the honor of caring for the sick and the welcoming of every distressed person. The fraternities kept for a long time the imprint of their beginnings and upon arriving in a place where there was still no friary, the friars stayed in the local hospitals or leprosaria and cared for the sick and the lepers. This care of the lepers was also the principal occupation of the candidates during their year of novitiate. The friars still worked with their hands between preaching, and some would gather food; others carried water ... Saint Francis had only forbidden activities and positions which would bring about the handling of money.

Uniformity also originated in the balance brought about between, on the one hand, the ideal unity summed up in a dynamic and short rule and, on the other hand, the juridical unity imposed by the constitutions and made all the more necessary because of the size and the international diffusion of the Order. The masterpiece of legislative flexibility, the Constitutions of Narbonne, were drawn up in 1260 by Saint Bonaventure. They condensed the accumulated experience of 40 years of living without weighing down or compromising the new initiatives and the evolution of the Order.

The Friars

Without becoming involved in a detailed and arcane nomenclature, it is still necessary to present several examples of the first generation Franciscans, simple friars, who are examples of faith and love, and others who are outstanding in study and preaching. Having incarnated the great gospel ideal at an important period in the history of the Church, they exerted a profound influence on their times.

Saint Francis sketched his portrait of an ideal friar as a composite of a group of his early companions. "The true Friar Minor," said the Saint, "should love poverty like Brother Bernard, should love prayer like Brother Rufino who prayed even while sleeping; he should be as lost in God as Brother

Giles, as courteous as Brother Angelo and as patient as Brother Juniper; he should possess the purity and the ingenuity of Brother Leo, the distinction and the good sense of Brother Masseo; and finally, representing detachment be like Brother Lucido who never stayed more than a month in the same place, under the pretext that on earth we have no lasting dwelling."

The relations between the first fraternities and their neighbors sometimes take on a charming aspect. At Greccio, in the evening, on the terrace after the day's work and preaching, the Brothers would sing one of the Laudes, or songs composed by Francis. Then, all the people of the town, in the gentleness of the Umbrian evening, left their homes scattered along the hillside and alternated the singing with the friars. They took up the refrain sung by all the echoes of the valley, "Be praised my Lord God!"

Alongside these simple and obscure friars, one can also find the great names of the Scholastics. From 1231 on, the fraternity of Paris counted among its members, a master, Alexander of Hales, a doctor of the secular clergy who became a friar and transferred his "chair" into his new cloister. This is how the friary of Paris, possessing from that time on a "chair of theology," became a university college, and attracted students from all over Europe. Alexander of Hales gave to Franciscan thought its first orientation along the lines of the Greek Fathers and gave to it an Augustinian coloration. Drawing his inspiration from Saint Francis, above everything else he put special emphasis on the goodness of God which presided at the creation of the universe and on the attraction to beauty which leads us back to God. Innocent IV ordered Alexander of Hales to condense his teaching into a book. In order to obey this command, Alexander of Hales published the first true"Summa of Theology," from whom Thomas Aquinas, his student, borrowed the form later on in his life.

Another Scholastic, John Fidanza, born in 1221 in a small Tuscan village, and miraculously cured from a mortal sickness through the intercession of Saint Francis, entered the Order at the age of twenty. Better known under the name of Saint Bonaventure, he studied at Paris under Alexander of Hales and in the company of Thomas Aquinas, received his doctorate in 1253, became the minister general of the Order at the age of thirty-six, bishop of Albano and cardinal at the age of fifty-two. He died during his attendance at the Council of Lyons in 1274. Among the numerous spiritual writings falsely attributed to him, but which were inspired by him, and give testimony to his prestige, the most important is the collection or compilation of the *Meditations on the Life of Christ* which for three centuries strongly influenced the art and spirituality of the entire West.

If Alexander of Hales is called the "Doctor Irrefragabilis" because of the unequaled solidity of his teaching, and Saint Bonaventure titled the "Doctor Seraphicus" for the mystical thrust of his doctrine, it is the title "Doctor Subtilis" which is given to John Duns Scotus (+1308). Ingenious and profound, he employed with unequaled panache all the sources of dialectics. It was the curious destiny of this Scotish Franciscan who studied at Paris and was forced out of Paris by Philip the Fair because he would not sign Philip's appeal against the pope, to die in Cologne at the age of thirty-five. He is especially known for the fullness of his Christocentric synthesis.

Roger Bacon is one of the founders of modern science, and one of the liveliest and most realistic scientists of his time. One of the early proponents of the experimental method, Bacon deepened the Franciscan love of creation through his scientific observation. He based his study of science on mathematics. He studied astronomy, optics, chemistry, and discovered phosphorus. It seems that he drew up plans for an airplane, of a steamboat, and of an immense bridge consisting of one arch. Two centuries before Columbus, he stated that, "in order to discover the shape of the earth it would be necessary to sail toward the West in order to arrive in the East." He knew Arabic, Greek, Hebrew, Chaldean, wishing to utilize all his knowledge in order to praise God, to understand Scripture, to know mankind, to help bring about the kingdom of God on earth. "A little science, " he said, "is able to distance one from God; a lot of knowledge leads you to him."

The list of the Franciscan masters of the 13th century is long but it is necessary to mention Jean de La Rochelle and Eudes Rigaud, John Peckham, and Matthew of Aquasparta . . .

At the same time, special attention is owed to a saint who became more renowned perhaps than Francis of Assisi, Saint Anthony of Padua. As a very young cleric, he was brought up in the scholasticate at the University of Lisbon and among the Augustinians of Coimbra, Portugal. One day in Lisbon, he attended the public reception of the bodies of the first five Franciscans martyred in Morocco, an experience which helped him decide on his true vocation; he joined the Franciscan Order. For eighteen months assigned very humble tasks in the friary, he then began a truly renowned career as a preacher throughout southern France and Italy, a public debater, a master of theology, and a true wonder-worker.

Uniting in himself a remarkable profane knowledge and sacred science, he enriched his sermons with numerous examples drawn from the life of plants and animals. He could be truly formidable when he defended the rights of the poor, and was the only one able to make the ferocious tyrant Ezzelino of Padua tremble. Saint Francis referred to Anthony as "my bishop." Popular devotion adopted Anthony of Padua as "the founder of lost objects."

The century does not draw to a close without the Third Order also furnishing and giving to the Church, Blessed

Angela of Foligno (1249-1309), a renowned mystic of great depth. Undergoing a conversion at the age of forty, she lived as a recluse and led a life of extraordinarily profound prayer. Her work *Teachings* is characterized by a luminous analysis of the life of prayer, by Christocentrism, and the primacy of love. Through her correspondence, she exercised an influence over numerous disciples, despite her secluded life.

The Arts

The influence of Francis of Assisi was felt also in the arts of the thirteenth century and the centuries that followed.

In poetry, he drew in his wake, the likes of Pacificus of Lisciano, who was crowned "king of poets" at the court of the emperor with the same crown that would later grace the heads of Petrarch and Tasso. Unfortunately, nothing remains of any of the works of this Franciscan troubadour.

Jacopone da Todi, like Francis, was born in Umbria and became a lawyer and a doctor at the University of Bologna. He was thirty-eight years old when the accidental death of his young wife turned him to a life of prayer and austerity. He entered the Friars Minor but refused the priesthood. This renowned lawyer also became a great poet, the most important and the best known of whose Latin works is a sequence, adopted into the Roman Liturgy, entitled *Stabat Mater,* which describes the sorrows of the Virgin at the foot of the Cross. He also composed more than a hundred "Laudes" in Umbrian—"dances of love and ballads of Paradise," in which all the genres are cultivated from the violent to the gentle, from the familiar to the supernatural.

"He dared to demand of his Christian faith," says 19th century author Frederick Ozanam, "not only truths to instruct men, but also beauty to delight them, not just readings, but also songs."

Architecture followed the same artistic lines. Over the tomb of Francis rose the great masterpiece of Italian Gothic art, the Basilica of Saint Francis in Assisi.

As for iconography, it would be exaggerated to say that a totally radical renovation of it was due to Francis and his disciples. But, at the same time it is certain that Francis and his disciples made all of Europe weep with their recitals of the passion, and they contributed to the advent of the touching and the sorrowful, born of their tender devotion to the humanity of Christ, and that, above all, characterized the new art from this point on.

The Poverello had only searched for the "kingdom of God and his justice" and he received in addition all the rest, specifically in regard to the magnificence of art used to portray him in the Basilica in Assisi. It is to Francis that the following century owes Dante and Giotto. "It is a strange thing," writes Renan, "that this sordid mendicant is the father of Italian art."

In France also, the person of Francis was quickly adopted by the medieval artists. Besides the quadrilobe enamel medallion of Limoges now in the museum of the Louvre and which dates from 1228-1230, shortly after the canonization of Francis, we have the opportunity also to see him placed in the first row of the elect in the Last Judgement of the Cathedrals of Amiens, Bourges, and Le Mans. In a corner of the cloister Mont Saint Michel he is portrayed as stigmatized, and this dates from 1228.

Already at the end of the thirteenth century, writes Father Agostino Gemelli, "Franciscanism has established itself as a spiritual force so completely that it has an influence on every social condition, and in every possible direction; in public places as well as in universities, in hermitages as well as in courts, among all European nations as well as upon the Asiatic hordes. This force is a concrete and activating love which gives to speculation a mystical thrust whose consequences are of extreme importance for action, for art, for civilization itself."

III.
The Fourteenth and Fifteenth Centuries

The first years of the fourteenth century saw the blossoming of *The Fioretti*. This masterpiece is the Italian version of an original Latin work entitled "The Acts of Saint Francis and his Companions." Found in *The Fioretti* are the activities and the daily life of some of the first fraternities. Their prayers, their preachings, and their travels, as well as the miracles and the penances of the friars, and the spontaneity of their relationships with each other are recorded here. An almost mystical inebriation mingled with good sense, a poetic approach mingled with concrete reality, a mixture of the sublime and the foolish, these are the secrets of the composition and attractiveness of *The Fioretti*.

But after the golden age of the first fraternities, there arose a stormy fourteenth century, which stands out against a sinister backdrop: 1337, the beginning of the Hundred Years' War; 1347, the Black Plague; 1378, the beginning of the Great Western Schism; and in Germany, battles between the Church and the Empire. These convulsive movements of Church and of society did not spare the Franciscan Order. It is significant that in the last eighty years of this century, the Order does not produce either a saint or a blessed for the Church.

The Battle Over Poverty

One hundred years after the beginning of the Order, the heroism of the first generations gives way to divisions and splits, particularly in the movement among some to observe poverty less rigorously. At the opposite end of the spectrum there are excesses of another minority, a minority that borders on heresy, because at times it ends up placing poverty above obedience, even obedience to the pope. These excesses on both sides only aggravate the situation. An open split breaks out when Pope John XXII imposes on the Order the ownership of its own friaries and that ownership is in common. It will be necessary to wait until the Council of Constance in 1415 in order to bring clarity to the situation by the beginnings of a movement called the Observance.

Among the representatives of a revolutionary mysticism, two authors who acquire a large audience particularly stand out: Angelo Clareno and Ubertino da Casale.

Angelo Clareno had the temperament of an agitator. He undertook the obligation of observing "to the letter and without gloss" the Rule and the Testament of Saint Francis. He wrote a *History of the Seven Tribulations of the Order of Minors,* whose title indicates the already polemical orientation of the book. He began an eremitical movement recognized by Pope Celestine V, but despite all his good intentions and particularly because of his obstinance, he ended up in prison and in exile and finally in exclusion from the Order. He persisted in continuing even after this and in considering himself the "general" of the Fraticelli, his own sect.

As for Ubertino da Casale, although he had a lively and quick-tempered spirit, he was a partisan of rigorism over charity and because of that he was exiled to LaVerna. There he composed in seven months a remarkable work, *Arbor Vitae Crucifixae Jesu,* or *The Tree of Life of the Crucified Jesus.*

Although it contains exceptional pages, worthy of the greatest mystics, it borders on apocalyptic outbursts against the Church and the popes, and even visions of a sixth age of the world marked by the return of Saint Francis and his struggle against the Antichrist.

Another important work of the time, but with a completely different orientation is *The Book of the Conformities of Blessed Francis with the Life of the Lord Jesus,* written by Friar Bartholomew of Pisa between 1385 and 1399. The author, already picked as a young cleric to be a student at Cambridge University, was not able to take up residence at that friary because of the Hundred Years War. Becoming a master in theology, he brought forth in this great work all the resemblances or similarities which make the life of Saint Francis an almost perfect imitation of the life of Christ. As an example, he uses the seal of the Order, the crossed arms over a bare cross—one the arm of Christ, the other the arm of the stigmatized Francis, as the very thesis of this book. Caught up with this parallelism, he can at times be somewhat arbitrary; but he wrote with intelligence and exactitude, his spiritual doctrine is solid and profound, and he utilized only biographical sources. The seal of the Order portrays today, as it always has, the crossed arms over a bare cross.

The Conformities met with success, but two centuries later they became a privileged target of the first Protestants. Erasmus Alber, master of a school in Saxony, wrote a pamphlet against *The Conformities* prefaced by Martin Luther and entitled "The Alcoran of the Franciscans."

In order to conclude this sad chapter of the quarrels in the Order, it is necessary to point out two things. In April, 1317, Pope John xxii accused seventy-two "Spirituals" of the friaries of Beziers and Narbonne of being insubordinate to the orders of the general, (among them was the celebrated friar Bernard Délicieux, the great adversary of the Inquisition) and had them brought to Avignon. In the course of the judicial process which lasted a year, only five of the accused held out to the end and were handed over to the secular authorities. Of the five unyielding friars, four were burned at the stake at Marseilles on the 7th of May, 1318, and the fifth one was condemned to life in prison.

Twenty years later, another papal intervention caused still more trouble in the Order. Benedict XII had belonged to the Cistercian Order and he now wished to give new constitutions to the Benedictines as well as to the Friars Minor. These constitutions, promulgated by the papal bull "Redemptor Noster," did not say a word about poverty, but insisted upon the obligation of choir, the obligation of silence and the enclosure, on the use of the dormitory, and on perpetual abstinence. The Chapter of Cahors recorded them, but it manifested its opposition in demanding deposition of the general who had obtained these constitutions. In 1354, another general, Guillaume Frainier, proposed new constitutions more conformable to the spirit of Saint Francis and to the traditions of the Order. The new constitutions were really the Constitutions of Narbonne with suitable amendments.

The Missions

One of the most beautiful pages in the Franciscan history of the fourteenth century is the story of the missions, even taking into account the darker moments such as the damages caused to Christianity by the revolution in China, the devastating invasion into Asia Minor by Tamerlane, and the bloody conquest of Bulgaria by Bajazet.

In Lithuania, the Franciscan apostolate began with the martyrdom of thirty-five friars who were massacred by the pagans at Vilna in 1325. Once again the blood of the martyrs was the seed of the Christian faith to which, this time, Duke Ladislaus converted in 1386. His people followed him.

In the Far East, it was Odoric of Pordenone who followed in the footsteps of John of Pian Carpino and John of Montecorvino. Setting out from Venice in 1314, he crossed Persia and Kurdistan, reaching eventually the Indian Ocean where he passed along the coast of Malabar. At one port call, he witnessed the bloody rites of a procession of Hindu idols. Later, following a long and complicated journey into the islands of Sonde, he arrived in China where he found several Franciscan houses with their Christian followers. An Italian colony had already been settled at Pekin. The Franciscan friary at Zayton, Ts' iuan—tcheou, opposite Formosa, already had a reception for the European merchants passing through the area. Odoric reached Tibet, and upon his return to Europe died the 14th of January, 1331.

In his account, he says naively, "I, myself, would not believe then if I had not seen with my own eyes and heard with my own ears everything that I now relate." And he confides in us his own astonishment: the friaries of Trebizonde, of Tana, and of Tauris in Armenia; the city of Sultanieh, capital of Persian Mongolia with its one hundred and twenty-five Christian churches, its Dominican archbishop and its Franciscan friary. He says of the Indian coasting vessels, "these boats are immense. They contain within them more than a hundred rooms and sometimes have more than 700 people on board. With a good wind, they can use up to ten tripartite sails which are very thick and which rarely break. These ships are marvelous things, despite their enormous size; there is no iron in the make-up, their walls and sides are not joined by any means of metal but are joined together with needle and thread and a kind of glue."

He talks about the fakirs of Meliapour, the chariot of Juggernaut, funeral pyres, conversations with the man-eating cannibals on the Isles of Andaman, and with the naked men of Nicobar. Between the Philippines and the Moluccas, he tells us that the current is very rapid. "The sea," he writes, "seems to be on a slope or an incline and runs with such violence that none would believe it. Our ship was in great danger." There is so much to relate, from fishing with cormorants, to the meal of the sacred monkeys, or his relations with the Buddhist priests, all the way to daily life in the friary of Pekin where he spent three years. And finally, his ministry in which over the course of thirty-three years of the apostolate he converted more than 20,000 pagans.

In the Near East, July 11, 1309, is an important date because of the permission granted to the Franciscans to reside in the Christian Holy Places. This permission was a "firman," a decree of Sultan Bibars who recognized the rights of the friars, and is still in force today. It is true that in 1363 persecution and martyrdom of the friars disturbed the peace, but the intervention of the European powers reestablished a relative calm in this province which was the flower of the Order since Saint Francis had gone there to follow in the footsteps of Christ. Since 1230, Pope Gregory IX had officially designated the friars as "The Guardians of the Holy Land."

It is not possible to pass over in silence the first attempt at "conversion of the crusades from violent methods to peaceful means" by the tertiary Raymond Lull. For him, it was not a question of driving Islam back by force of arms. "It is necessary," he says, "to know Islam in order to understand it, and to love it in order to conquer it." Raymond was a Catalan nobleman who converted, then spent nine years in learning Arabic, philosophy, and theology. He acquired at Montpellier the title of master and obtained from the king the foundation of Miramar, a college of languages, where thirteen friars were prepared for the evangelization of the infidels through the study of Arabic.

Raymond met with princes and prelates from throughout Christianity in order to interest them in his great missionary endeavor. He preached in all the synagogues and mosques of Spain. He undertook two voyages to Africa, Tunisia, and Bougie. Everywhere, he found the time to fight against the Averroist theories and wrote numerous works. He himself translated into Arabic his own book *The Great Art.* He taught at Paris and assisted at the Council of Vienne (1311-1312) where, under his inspiration, the council decreed the foundation of several chairs of languages: Arabic, Greek, Hebrew, and Chaldean at the Universities of Paris, Oxford, Bologna, and Salamanca.

He ended his life, almost an octogenarian, by the drawing up of fifteen collections of controversies and by one last apostolic voyage to Tunisia, Algeria, Bone, and Bougie, where he was almost stoned to death. What a career! This great missionary had undertaken and put into operation the idea, inaugurated by Saint Francis at Damietta, of the peaceful crusade "through preaching and through the blood of the martyrs."

The Great Plague

The Black Death of 1347, which decimated Europe, occasioned the sanctity of another Franciscan tertiary, Roch of Montpellier. In the course of a pilgrimage to Rome he stayed in the hospitals where he took care of those stricken by the plague and sometimes cured them with the sign of the Cross. Having himself contracted the plague, he would have died alone in the woods if a little dog had not come to lick his wounds and bring him bread each day. Once cured, he took to the roads as a pilgrim-healer.

The moral and social ravages of the Great Plague were more serious than the sufferings and the funeral processions. The great slaughter was of serious import for the future of Europe. In Italy, it is estimated that ten thousand Friars Minor perished during the plague. At Marseilles and at Carcasonne, all the friars died without exception. Mariano of Florence estimates that the Order was reduced by one third of its total numbers.

The scourge having passed, a certain laxity and looseness was found in the friaries which the friars could not bring themselves to abandon. Besides, in order to fill the empty places there began a "chase after vocations." Candidates were sought through the promise of material advantages and ecclesiastical positions. From 1312 to 1415, a little more than a hundred years, 568 Franciscans became bishops! The Rule became intolerable to these new recruits. Many superiors favored disorganization, exclaustration, and the acquiring of sometimes considerable goods.

As a crowning misfortune, a good part of Europe underwent the Hundred Years War. A great number of friaries, situated in the suburbs of the cities, were prey to the troops passing through. Other friaries were destroyed for strategic reasons, to prevent the enemy from fortifying them or from transforming them into strategic bases of attack against the city. In the process, the friary of Sens disappeared. Some religious took refuge in neighboring friaries, but others simply rejoined their families; many others took to the road and joined the great number of vagabonds. With this break, the beautiful ideal of fraternity at the service of the Church seemed to disappear.

The Fifteenth Century

The fifteenth century provided the Order with the atmosphere and the framework for a new beginning and a restructuring.

Nevertheless, this new century began rather poorly with the repercussions of the Great Western Schism and the struggle between three popes which was felt in all the religious families. There were three concurrent popes in the Church, and three generals for the Franciscan Order. Poverty was the first casualty, because the popes, in order to keep and gain adherents, distributed great revenues and accorded many privileges. And obedience, how to practice it when three superiors commanded contradictorily and excommunicated and deposed those who did not obey?

The seed of reform had already been planted, and began to develop with Blessed Paul Trinci at the hermitage of Bruliano near Foligno. His was a true reform, which was to renew and not to break apart.

The real promoter of this reform of the Observance was Saint Bernardine of Siena. When he took the habit in 1402, twenty-five small friaries in Italy had already rallied around the reform. Bernardine himself established three hundred friaries, housing four thousand friars. Ten years after his death, the Observants had reached the number of twenty thousand.

The Conventuals, in response to the Observant Reform, regrouped. They did not renounce the concessions accorded them by the sovereign pontiffs, which conferred on them the right to possess goods and receive stable revenues. A first step towards the separation between the two branches was the nomination of vicars general proper to the Observants in 1443. It will be necessary to wait, however, for the papal bull of Leo x in 1517, *Ite et Vos in Vineam Meam,* to juridically consecrate the separation which in fact already existed.

The Action of the First Order

There were three predominant preachers of the Franciscan Order in the fifteenth century.

First and foremost is Saint Bernardine of Siena, counsellor of popes and of political leaders, and promoter of devotion to the Holy Name of Jesus. We have the texts of his numerous sermons; their very rich language is a harbinger of the Renaissance. His sermons combine classical and patristic erudition but at the same time are models of simplicity.

His doctrine, thoroughly Franciscan, is based on the principles: "God is love, knowledge is love, duty is love, and paradise is love." But with even this gentle philosophy he can also thunder against luxury and against gambling, the two scourges of the period. After hearing him preach at Bologna, the players all came to bring their dice, their chessboards, all their instruments of gambling, and made of them a bonfire. At Bologna, the people raised a pyre on which all the women threw their jewels, their wigs, their watered perfumes, garlands, high-heels, and "other paraphernalia." Bernardine could speak of business and the eighteen sins one can commit (no fewer than eighteen) in conducting business. Another time he can paint a beautiful and graceful picture of a cheerful home. At another time he would preach in one of those prophetic accents with which Savanarola would later terrify Florence.

Here is a story which Saint Bernardine often told. It is entitled, "The Old Friar, the Novice, and the Ass."

"Once upon a time a holy friar, prudent and circumspect in all the things of the world, had observed that no behavior is able to escape criticism. He spoke one day to one of the young novices. 'Son, take our little donkey and come with me.' The obedient novice untied the donkey and the old friar mounted the donkey while the novice followed on foot.

In a very muddy area of the road they passed through a group of people. One of the onlookers cried out, 'Oh! Look! What a mean old monk. He lets the poor young novice walk through the mud while he relaxes and takes it easy on the back of the donkey.' Scarcely had the old religious heard these words than he stopped the donkey, got down, and put the young novice in his place while he walked in the mud goading the donkey on from behind. Another one of the onlookers exclaimed, 'What a strange man! At his age he walks in the mud, and puts this strong and sturdy young monk who has no care whether he is tired or muddy. He must be crazy. It would be better for both of them to ride on the donkey.' Then the holy old man climbed up on the donkey too. But a little further on, another onlooker observed, 'Look at those two on the donkey. What do they care about the donkey. He could die from all this.' Hearing this, the holy old friar immediately got down, had the novice also get down, and they both walked one behind the other crying to the donkey, 'Move it! Move it' A little further down the road, another onlooker cried out, 'Look at these crazy and ridiculous people! They have a donkey, and here they are walking through the mud.' The holy old friar then turned and said to the young novice, 'Let us go back to the friary.' Once in his cell, he said to the novice, 'Did you pay close attention to the teaching of the donkey? Realize that in this world all the good you do, and no matter how you use and employ all your strength, no matter what, you will never be able to avoid being condemned. Avoid the world then, and whether it be for good or for evil, allow whoever wants to speak to say what they want.'"

Like Bernardine of Siena, Saint John Capistran walked all over Europe in order to spread devotion to the Holy Name of Jesus. He had the monogram of the Holy Name attached to his military banners. The taking of Constantinople by the Turks in 1453, found John Capistran as Nuncio and Inquisitor in Germany where he organized the crusade. He even directed the naval combat on the Danube in order to save Belgrade which was being besieged by Mahomet II in 1456.

Saint James of the Marches was also a fighter for a cause, but without the excesses of temperament of a warrior, and was named by Rome as the papal legate against all the heresies and schisms which arose during this time. His persuasive force worked marvels in this area especially in Norway, Pomerania, Bohemia, and Hungary.

In France, the name of Richard le Cordelier should be remembered, first as the confessor of Joan of Arc. He followed her onto the battlefield at Orleans and at Rheims. It was at his suggestion that she had the monogram of the Holy Name painted on her standard, which is also the last word she pronounced as she was being burned at the stake. He is also known for the power of his sermons, which sometimes lasted five hours! According to a *Diary of a Middle Class Person of Paris,* "he was responsible for turning more people to devotion than all the preachers who had tried for a hundred years."

Friar Jean Bourgeois also attracted great crowds. Besides, he so enchanted Charles VIII, that he was chosen as the royal counsellor, and Charles insisted Friar Jean baptize the Dauphin. When Rabelais would later speak about a popular preacher, he could only compare him to "little Friar Jean Bourgeois."

Olivier Maillard was another outstanding preacher who planted the seed of the gospel all across France, from Albi to Bruges, and from Nantes to the border of the Rhine. This Breton friar graduated from the University of Paris and became vicar general of the Observants. His sermons, resting on broad knowledge and solid scriptural foudations, attracted great crowds during the 42 years of his career as a preacher. His popularity rested on his grace and vigor and sometimes the tartness of his language. He grappled with all the ecclesiastical abuses of his age. He met head on the vices of accumulation of benefices and traffic in indulgences. He inveighed against usurers, judges, profligates, and drinkers.

Olivier Maillard, and with him, his contemporaries such as Antoine Fradin and Michel Menot, stayed well within the context of Franciscan preaching. Friar Olivier explained dogma conscientiously, with knowledge and profound realism, but in simple terms. He was at ease preaching in the area of morals as well. During an entire Lent in Paris, he centered his sermons on the vices. He knew how to choose striking examples and was never as severe in thundering as when he took up the defense of the poor and the oppressed, sometimes leaving the pulpit to dig jibes at the people in their seats. Popular preaching, yes; but it gave the common people the courage to be faithful Christians as well as take pride in living good lives. Of Friar Michel Menot, whose sermons are a rich mine of knowledge of the daily life of the time, let us cite this beautiful saying which helps reveal his general tone. "These Lords of Justice who sport long and beautiful robes, with their wives clothed like princesses, oh, if their robes would pass through the presses, the blood of the poor would flow from them."

All these preachers belonged to the people and maintained permanent contact with them. "They are always outside," wrote Imbart de la Tour, "at the crossroads or in the streets; they speak to everyone, they sing in public, they take care of the sick, they run to put out fires; they help with their hands in giving bread to those who need it . . . and the people love them. The crowds want them to preach. They want them to pray, they want them to bring them to pray . . . . The friars are indeed the yeast that works through the dough."

Theologians and Mystics

During this period, one can search in vain for a savant comparable to the doctors of the preceding century. Two theologians, however, merit special attention, Blessed Angelo de Chivasso (+1459), the author of a magnificent *Summa* of cases of conscience, which Martin Luther mocked, and Friar Thierry Coelde of Munster (+1515), the author of *Mirror of a Christian*, a solid and clear catechetical instruction, the oldest in the German language.

In the area of Sacred Scripture, the Franciscan Ximenes, cardinal and regent of Spain, who had his celebrated *Biblia Complutensis* published (a polyglot Bible, edited by the University of Alcala in 1517, a university which he had founded). On the order of Louis XI, Friar William le Menan translated the Bible into French around 1484. He also translated the *Life of Christ* by Ludolph le Chartreux.

In the great constellation of spiritual authors in the Rheno-Flemish school (such as Ruysbroeck, Tauler, and Eckhart), a friar stands out with particular brilliance: Henry Harphius or de Harp (+1477). Guardian of the friary at Malines, this mystic was a renowned preacher, important for his written work. His influence was still felt two centuries later as much in the Order as without, both inside and outside of his own country. A certain lack of precision and of prudence in the use of mystical vocabulary earned him many troubles with the Roman censor, but quite quickly the editions of his work were corrected and served as the official works for the teaching of mystical theology in the friaries, especially in Spain, the Low Countries, and in Italy.

The accomplishments of Friar Jehan Tisserant should be mentioned. A doctor in theology at the University of Paris, and at the same time a popular preacher, he was the confessor of Queen Anne of Brittany, and founder in 1492 of the Refuge Saint-Madeleine for repentant prostitutes, the

Madelonnettes. He is also known as a musician, as a composer of Christmas carols, and of sequences or poetry in
Latin, the most celebrated of these is without doubt "O Filii
et Filiae."

The Poor Clares

As the First Order continued its reform with Saint
Bernardine of Siena, so also the Second Order underwent
reform, due to the initiative of a carpenter's daughter born
in 1381 in Corbie—Nicolette Boylet, called simply, Colette.
In 1408, she undertook to renew and reform her monastery
of Besancon. Her influence, with the help of Benedict XIII
whom she had met at Nice, won her more and more followers and she even extended her influence over the friars.
Colette was a remarkable, intelligent, and decisive woman.
Popes, kings, princes and prelates, respected her sugges-
tions.

She passed easily from the territory of the Armagnacs
to the territory of the Bourguignons. The bands of "Scorch-
ers" who ran through France at the time always respected
the carriage of the Abbess of Besancon. A letter signed by
Sister Colette was the best safe-conduct. "Always on the
road," says Claudel, "Colette, like a diligent needle, travels
across a torn-apart France, and sews up the pieces with
charity." Her activity is parallel to that of Joan of Arc. Joan
was still in the cradle, according to a legend, when Colette,
passing through Domremy, blessed her and gave her a ring
engraved with the names of Jesus and Mary as a gift.

Within forty years she established fifteen monasteries
and those which she reformed are innumerable. The Church
had to wait for a Theresa of Avila in order to find a like-
minded temperament and a similar success in religious
reform.

The Beginnings of Humanism

The ferment of humanism (the philosophical and literary movement in which human values and capabilities are the focus), which worked its way across Europe, also worked its way among the Franciscans.

If certain friaries forbade the study of Greek as opening the door to freedom of thought, Rabelais and his superior of the friary of Fontenay undertook a correspondence with Guillaume Bude, the great humanist, as revenge. Jean Vitrier, the guardian of the friary of Saint-Omer was a remarkable professor. The Dutchman Erasmus, a great figure of the Renaissance, has left us an admirable portrait of him. It was Jean Vitrier who said, "It would be a sin to persist in exaggerated fasts and for a question of food and money to compromise their sacred studies." Another friend of Erasmus, a renowned Hebrew scholar, but one who passed over to Lutheranism, was Conrad Pellikan, guardian of the friary of Basle. Bude himself wrote in his letter to Rabelais that he has received news through "one of the most cultivated members of the Order." This testimony proves that all the friars were not as ignorant nor as reactionary as those who confiscated Greek books and censured Erasmus.

Franciscans were involved in humanism on an equal footing with other scholars. Not only did they retain the taste and the traditions for study from their great ancestors of the thirteenth century, (Bernardine of Siena suggested joining the study of Cicero with that of Saint Jerome; Albert of Sarteano wrote beautiful Latin; James of the Marches, the first great "Dantologue," founded at Monteprandone one of the richest libraries of the fifteenth century), but the Franciscans had a sharp sense for the dignity and the promotion of the person and the value of individual conscience. In the question of free will, they knew how to reconcile the respect for human initiative with grace. Many Franciscans upheld, as a family tradition, the cult of beauty inherited from their founder who was a poet. The friaries of the fifteenth century are remarkable for their charm no less than for their simplicity and their decoration. In Italy, for example, friaries were decorated with Della Robbias or Donatello sculptures, all of which is witness to a love of beauty and a strengthening optimism.

Even those engaged in politics knew how to redeem or disengage meanness or pettiness from a narrow nationalism. One example of this is Friar Jean Glapion, confessor to Charles v. He was a man of rare finesse, and Erasmus, in one of his letters, congratulates the emperor for having as his counsellor such a religious, who is exempt from the passions of this world, and has only the general interest and the glory of Christ in mind.

It is true that among the ranks of the friars, one can also find certain moralists who are grumpy or crabbed in their thought. Some of them, in the name of simplicity or austerity, lump together in the same condemnation heretical pride and classical studies, sensuality and art. It is true, for example, that Pierre le Cornu, and Francis Titelman, professor of Sacred Scripture at Louvain, railed against the great Erasmus. Nicholas Herborn, vicar of the Ultramontanes, said, "Erasmus laid the eggs, Luther hatched them." Erasmus replied, "Saint Francis became great before everyone not by slander or back-biting, but by virtue . . . one does not imitate Francis because he goes barefoot, wears a woolen cord, or a religious habit . . . I have fought abuses and prejudices everywhere they are found, but I have never attacked any religious order. I have only prosecuted or gone after the judaic exaggerations of certain monks who have more respect for the Rule of Saint Francis than they do for the gospel."

Apart from these exceptions, the sons and daughters of Saint Francis in general felt themselves at ease in the humanist current and did not consider as "pagan" a world coming from the hands of God. They wished to accept it integrally in order to make it integrally Christian. They added "knowledge and science so that science does not become the ruin of the soul."

IV.
The Sixteenth Century

Tension in Paris

As the 16th century dawned, a religious revolution began within the Church and various intellectual and spiritual currents agitated the Order and provoked "disturbances" particularly in the great urban centers. These repercussions were felt throughout the Order. The Reformation was at hand. Within the Franciscans sub-groups were formed as a craving for change spread throughout Europe.

At Paris, for example, various attempts at reform collided with the most determined and the most quaint oppositions. A contemporary chronicler has left us a rather vivid account. Here are the basic facts. In 1502, Olivier Maillard, then vicar general, for the third time, of the Ultramontane (a formal term meaning North of the Alps—literally: beyond the mountains), Observants tried to introduce into the friary at Paris fifty new friars acquired for the reform. They were to be the kernel and the nucleus of the reform at Paris. We already know that at this date, through the testimony of Conrad Pellikan, that there were three-hundred and fifty young friars studying in the friary at Paris. Fifty new friars acquired for the reform? No, the community refused to accept them. On the order of Georges D' Amboise, the cardinal legate, two bishops attempted a solemn visit in order to impose the reform on the friary. At the news of their arrival, the friars exposed the Blessed Sacrament on the altar and began the divine office. When the bishops made their entrance, the choir intoned, "Adjuva nos, Deus, salutaris noster!" meaning "Help us, O God, our Savior!" And at each attempt of the two prelates to begin their announcement, a new psalm was intoned. After four hours of this liturgical obstruction, the bishops beat a hasty retreat.

They returned the following day, and this time the bishops were accompanied by an officer of the king and a hundred archers. The sight of the archers brought prudence to the friars who did not attempt a repeat of the previous evening; the bishops were able to promulgate the application of the reform. But so many doctors present were not caught napping. "They defended their side," says the Chronicler, "in showing titles, rules, authorities, reasons and examples, dispensations and privileges, and all the rights and privileges which were able to help them." Finally, a commission was appointed in order to "study the terms and conditions of the reform." Naming a commission really meant the whole affair ended in failure. This was the climate of farce and tension in which important events in the history of the Church unfolded. Rabelais will remember it—thirty years later, his monks of Seuille (in his *Gargantua,* XXVIII) will attempt the same methods of plain-chant as their brothers in Paris.

The Situation in the Order

This little episode demonstrates how urgent it was to clarify the situation within the Order, made even more confused by the proliferation of so many reforms and subgroups. The goal and purpose of the papal bull of Leo X *Ite et Vos in Vineam Meam,* of May 29th, 1517, was to clarify the situation within the Order.

This bull is one of division since it formally consecrated the separation between the Conventuals and the

Observants; but it is also a bull of union since it brought together under a single authority and in obedience to the same constitutions all the Observants, Amedeans, Clareni, Colettines, and other minor reforms. But union did not imply uniformity. The Order was not yet ripe for a monolithic or centralized government. Not only did these small groups keep a certain independence, but there were also attempts to create new ones. Besides maintaining a geographical division which had divided the Observants into the Cismontanes and the Ultramontanes (meaning this side of the mountains and beyond the mountains, the Alps), there was still another division between the Regular Observance and the Strict Observance! And among the Strict Observance, there were new reforms and new sub-divisions.

The Recollects were primarily religious who lived in friaries called "Friaries of Recollection," in order to give themselves over to contemplation more than to the apostolate. The General Chapter of 1402 had provided for at least one Friary of Recollection in each province. In 1571, the friary of Rabastens in Aquitaine provided the impetus for a vast movement which extended rapidly throughout France, to Portugal and Spain, which went so far as to form separate provinces. Then it spread to Germany, to Belgium, and to Canada. At the end of the seventeenth century, the Recollects numbered four-hundred and fifty friaries, and more than ten thousand religious.

The Alcantarines were born and took shape in the religious climate of Spain. Their head and founder was Saint Peter of Alcantara (+1562), whose extraordinary and unparalleled austerity gave its stamp to the entire branch. They numbered four-thousand six-hundred by the year 1700. Then came the Reformati, who from their beginning were often confused with the Discalceati. They began in Italy around 1525 and their friaries soon covered the entire peninsula.

It is necessary to understand that the proliferation of these many reforms did not prevent or hinder the growth of the main branch itself, since, in the following century there were over 64,400 Observants in general—34,900 belonged to the Regular Observance, and the rest belonged to the sub-groups recently founded.

The Capuchins

And if this was not enough, the evangelical dynamism of the Church in the 16th century brought about even another more original and important reform, the Capuchins.

Around 1525, a friar of the Observance, Matthew da Baschi, received from Clement VII the authorization to lead an eremitical form of life, living like hermits. He was joined by several companions and in 1529 drew up statutes which the pope approved. They took the name of "the Friars Minor of the Eremitical Life," a name which was quickly transformed into the popular name of Capuchins because of the particular form of the capuche (hood) which was sewn to their habit. Their friaries were to be situated outside of the cities and would have no more than twelve religious in each friary. The counsels of poverty contained in the Rule of Saint Francis would be applied in all their rigor. Despite some initial setbacks, the Capuchins in Italy made considerable progress due as much to the manner of their preaching as to the example of their life of prayer and their universal charity, especially during the epidemics and plagues.

Their substantial growth dates from 1574, when Gregory XIII allowed them to expand outside of Italy, to France, Switzerland, and Germany, where they were received and welcomed with enthusiasm. In 1625 they numbered 17,000 and in 1745, 32,000. For a long time, they were governed by a vicar general dependent upon the minister general of the Conventuals. In 1619, Pope Paul v made them independent and gave them their own minister general. Ultimately, then, the Order found itself divided into three large autonomous families: the Conventuals, the Capuchins, and the Observants, with the Observants being divided into several more groups of which the more important ones were the Recollects, the Alcantarines, and the Reformati.

The Protestant Reform

The mendicant friars were the special target of the Protestant movement both for controversy as well as for persecution. Already in the 14th century, John Wyclif had attacked not only the privileges but even the legitimacy of these religious and the value of their vows. Luther had written the preface for the pamphlet entitled "The Alcoran of the Friars." Luther then drew up two series of theses against the vows.

The battle became open persecution between Protestants and Catholics. In Germany and in Austria 300 friaries were confiscated or destroyed. Four hundred and sixty Franciscans were martyred for the faith between 1520 and 1620. In England, the friars were banished, considered criminals, and were burned at the stake. The first of these was John Forest, confessor to Queen Catherine of Aragon, whom Henry VIII wished to repudiate in order to marry Ann Boleyn. In the Low Countries in 1572, at Gorcum, Nicholas, the guardian, and the entire community were tortured and then killed, for their belief in the Real Presence and for their fidelity to the pope.

France was not spared, and the names of the victims reads like a long list of martyrs. At Vezelay, for example, in

1568, at the friary of LaCordelle which had been founded during the lifetime of Francis, the heads of the martyred friars served in a sinister game of "quilles" (similar to bowling) whose target was the head of the guardian who had been buried alive with only his head sticking out of the ground. At Orleans, six religious were poisoned in their prison. At Angouleme, the guardian of the friary, Michel Grelet, was hanged from a tree in the presence of Admiral Coligny. Brother Viroleau was mutilated and put to death. Brother Avril, eighty years old, had his head split in two by the blow of a halberd. In the provinces of the north of France and in Flanders, twenty-four friaries were destroyed; fifty-seven friaries for the two provinces of Aquitaine.

It was necessary to react, and the first and foremost goal was to reform the Order from within. The wealth of the Church having often served as pretext for revolt, the first mission of the sons of the Poverello was to give witness to evangelical poverty. Even on the point of traffic in indulgences, several strong and clear positions were taken. The guardian of the friary of Mainz declined the position of being comissary general for the preaching of the indulgence. The minister general himself, Quinones, obtained from the pope in 1520 permission for the friars to be dispensed from preaching on indulgences attached to the collection of alms and money.

Another general of the Friars Minor, Francois Lychet, understood the necessity of providing a solid foundation for preachers; and the Protestant Reform thus paradoxically led to the beginnings of a renewal of theology and preaching. This Francois Lychet was one of the great generals of the Order, his generalate distinguished for the far-reaching effects of certain of his projects as well as by his attention to all the details. He understood that authority cannot simply be content with giving directives, but must also carefully watch over the execution of these directives. He

deposed seventy-two guardians because they did not suffi-
ciently take care of the sick brothers. He died on the 15th of
September, 1520, at Buda in the course of a tour of inspec-
tion of the Order in Hungary. The urgent need for serious renewal in preaching was pressed and had to be universal. In
1521, the bishop of Meaux, after having visited the 320
parishes of his diocese, was able to find only fourteen
priests among all his clergy who were prepared and capable
of preaching the word of God. One of the great needs was a
better preparation of the clergy for preaching.

The general chapter of 1521 passed this regulation,
"As it is our duty to offer ourselves intrepidly through
spiritual arms against the adversaries of the Church who
deny the faith, the minister general and the chapter order
all, first, to have recourse to prayer . . ., and to resist heresy
even to the shedding of the blood if it is necessary, and in
preaching the word of God and cultivating holy theology."
The program was solid and simple, but vast, and it was
applied.

In the Second Order several heroines of the Counter-
Reform are also found. The Poor Clares of the ancient and
renowned monastery of Nuremburg suffered much. Former
Augustinians who had transferred to the Rule of Saint Clare
in 1274, at the time of the Reformation they numbered sixty.

The Abbess, Charitas Pirkheimer, was a woman of
great culture and sanctity. Her father was an ambassador,
her brother was a friend of Erasmus and of the leading
Protestant reformer, Melancthon. She herself knew patrol-
ogy (the study of the early Church Fathers), read Saint
Jerome freely, and participated in the theological confron-
tations of the period. When Jerome Emser wrote polemics
against Luther in 1523, she wrote the author to congratulate
him. Unfortunately, her letter fell into the hands of the
reformers who published it.

Then the misfortunes of the monastery began. The

council of the city ceased it subsidies and grants which it had been bound to furnish since the foundation of the monastery. Then came the moral vexations. The nuns were forbidden to address themselves to the Franciscans, and were under the obligation of confessing themselves to preachers of the reformation. Four of these reform preachers were installed by force in the monastery, and the sisters were to submit to their preaching. They were forbidden to wear the religious habit; the cloister was abolished. For five years the sisters lived in absolute poverty; for five years they were deprived of Mass and Communion. What persecution had been unable to do, time and sickness finally was able to achieve.

Father Gilbert-Nicholas, better known under the name of Father Gabriel-Maria, which had been given to him by Leo x because of his great devotion to the mystery of the Annunciation, was counsellor to the Queen-Mother Louise of Savoy and spiritual director of Jeanne of France. He expounded to the faculty of Paris, gathered in solemn convocation the 7th of October, 1523, the articles of faith placed in doubt by the new theories of Lutheranism.

The friar Giles Cailleau who gave extreme unction to Marguerite of Navarre, sister of Francis I, saw himself assigned by the minister general to the region of Libourne and Bordeaux where his preaching worked wonders for the defense of orthodoxy.

At Vannes, it was Brother Olivier de France, doctor of the University of Nantes, who was chosen in 1563 to be the first theologian of the cathedral chapter since there was no proper and competent canon, who defended the faith.

Other preachers also worked efficaciously: at Tours, Pierre Bourgogne; at Avallon, François Marcou; at Orleans, Maurice Hilaret; all three doctors from Paris. The friary of Metz distinguished itself by its active resistance to heresy, in particular a certain Father Fidelis who confounded the leading Protestant reformer, William Farel, in public debate.

Father Angelo Justiniani, commisary of the Order for all of France, participated in the Colloquium of Poissy in 1560 where his perfect knowledge of Greek (his mother tongue) allowed him to correct this or that erroneous interpretation of Theodore of Beze. Angelo became the bishop of Geneva following this.

One episode is characteristic of the general climate of this period. It was during Lent, 1563, so an unnamed chronicler tells us, at La Sainte Chapelle in Paris. "A priest was singing High Mass. In the front row of those assisting was a Huguenot (Protestant French follower of John Calvin), imitating a good Catholic, genuflecting, signing himself with the Sign of the Cross like the others. But, after the consecration, the Huguenot jumped up, grabbed the Host, threw it on the ground and stepped on it. After a moment of astonishment, the crowd reacted to this sacrilege by hitting the offender with blows of the fist and kicking him and then handing him over to the justice of the Parliament, which condemned him to having his hand cut off, and then being burned alive. In order to save at least his soul, Father Jean Barrier, guardian of the friars of Provins and theologian of Saint-Quiriace, was sent to him. The prisoner asked pardon for his sin and for all his other sins, and the friar implored from his pulpit for his listeners to pray for this man."

Theology

The great importance given to theology because of the Reformation and the Counter-Reformation was very beneficial for Franciscan thought and theology—strengthened and supported by the theologians of the newly founded Society of Jesus. One hundred and three theologians of the Franciscan Order were called as experts to the Council of

Trent, and Franciscan theologians were very active in its deliberations.

The optimism of Franciscan theology as evidenced in Christocentrism and the primacy of the will through the thrust of love were reconciled with the problems of grace and free will and were approved by the Council. Some members of the Order who achieved renown for themselves and the Franciscan movement were: Alphonse of Castro (+1558); François Feuardent (+1612); Noel Taillepied (+1558), a friar from Pontoise in France and the author of the *Lives of Luther, Carolstadt, and Peter the Martyr*. The general of the Order, Christopher of Cheffontaine (+1559), was the author of a number of works, among them, a tract entitled *Defense of the Faith*.

Among the Franciscans and Carmelites of the sixteenth century, spiritual and mystical theology were almost entirely centered in Spain. The great Saint Teresa of Avila (+1582) recognized her good fortune in having as guides and masters several outstanding authors of the Franciscan Order: Alphonse of Madrid and his *Art of Serving God*; Francis of Osuna, whose *Spiritual Primer* Teresa acknowledged having read and used for her meditations; Bernardine of Laredo whose *Ascension of Mount Sion* Teresa stated she read and from it derived great profit, and St. Peter of Alcantara.

Here is the portrait of Saint Peter of Alcantara, drawn by the celebrated reformer of Carmel, Teresa, his penitent: "Among other austerities, for twenty years he wore a hair shirt of pieces of iron without ever taking it off. He spent forty years without sleeping more than an hour and a half a day. Of all his mortifications, that which cost him the most in the beginning was that of conquering the need for sleep. For this purpose he always knelt or remained standing and the little sleep that he did allow himself, he always took seated. Even if he had had a desire to lie down, he would not have been able to because his cell was only four and a half feet long. Never did he wear shoes. He had only one habit, and that of heavy wool. He ate only once every three days; and as I seemed surprised at this, he said that this was easy to anyone who had made it a habit. One of his companions assured me that sometimes he would go on for eight days without taking any nourishment. His body was so thin that he seemed to be made of the roots of trees. But , with all his holiness and sanctity he was always affable. Soundness and the graces of his spirit gave to his words I know not what irresistible charm."

The Capuchin school counted among its great masters, Benedict of Canfield whose original name was William Fitch, an Englishman, converted from Puritanism, who died at the beginning of the following century in 1610. He was favored with exceptional mystical graces and his *Rule of Perfection* showed, without falling into Quietism, (a heresy that God did everything and you simply remained passive), how all sanctity leads one to do the will of God and of allowing oneself to be led by him.

The Missions

The work of the Franciscan missionaries continued uninterrupted in all the territories already cultivated during the preceding century. It is the Japanese missions which especially stand out during the sixteenth century, particularly Christianity in Nagasaki, where the persecutions and martyrdoms in 1597 only brought forth new converts. The mission in the Philippines with its colleges and leprosaria is one of the most flourishing. It was equaled only by that of the Indies, where the first Archbishop of Goa was the outstanding Friar Jean Albuquerque, viceroy of the East Indies, who gave to his Christians an extraordinary impetus. Moreover, it was he who welcomed and helped Saint Francis Xavier on his first missionary trip to India.

An entirely new field of activity was opened to the missionaries, the recently discovered New World. The planting of the faith and the Church in these countries was made more difficult by the fact that the colonizers, coming from Christian nations, sometimes gave counter witness to the faith by their political, financial, and even religious rivalries, to say nothing of their morals and their cruelty.

The first bishops of the Americas were Franciscans. Bernard Boyl, a Catalan, first a Benedictine hermit at Montserrat, then a Minim, then a friar, and confidant of the king of Spain, was nominated by Alexander VI on the 25th of June, 1493, in the bull "Piis Fidelium" and given vast canonical powers for the Americas. There was Jean Garcia Padilla, bishop of Haiti in 1504 and Jean de Aquevedo of Santa Maria la Antiqua on the Gulf of Darien, Colombia, in 1514.

The first priest to have the joy of celebrating the Sacrifice of the Mass in America was Father Juan Perez de Marchena, guardian of the Friary of La Rabida, a friend and counselor of Columbus. It was also a Franciscan, Friar Bernard Cousin, who was the first martyred in America. He was shot through with arrows on the 18th of January, 1585, at Guadeloupe.

Cortez, on several occasions, had asked the emperor to send him some religious for New Spain. In 1524, the first mission, composed of Franciscans, arrived. There were a dozen, as with the Apostles. An eyewitness, Bernard Diaz, has left us an account of their arrival in Mexico.

"When Cortez knew that they had arrived," writes Diaz, "he got down off his horse, walked forward to meet the twelve pilgrims, and was the first to kneel before Friar Martin of Valencia and tried to kiss his hand. But Friar Martin refused to allow him to do so. Cortez kissed his habit, and also that of all the other friars, and we also did the same, all the captains and the soldiers present. When the Indians saw Cortez kneel and try to kiss the hands of Friar Martin, they were astounded. When they looked at the friars, bare-foot, thin, with torn habits, not on horse but on foot, and kneeling before them Cortez, whom they took for a god like one of their gods, they followed his example and from that point on they received the friars with similar respect."

The great name in the American mission at this time is Juan de Zumarraga, the pioneer of Mexico, called Protector of the Indians. Named by Clement VII to the episcopal see of Mexico in 1530, he brought missionaries from Spain, and even brought the Poor Clares. Giving all his attention to the work of education, he established over a hundred schools, which up to 70,000 children attended. He drew up a sort of catechism in the language of the Indians, translated the New Testament into Aztec, and set up in Mexico the first printing press in the Americas. In 1536, he even built a seminary which later was transformed into a university which was destined to enjoy a brilliant career up to the Mexican Revolution of 1911.

A large number of friars became linguists and inter-viewers for the purpose of knowing their flock better and to root out the pre-Hispanic pagan religions. "Among knowl-edgeable researchers of the precortesian civilization," writes modern historian Professor R. Ricard, "it is necessary to single out the illustrious Franciscan Bernardin de Sahagun who can justly be considered a precursor of modern ethnol-ogy. Sahagun, in effect, was not only a specialist fluent in the 'Nahuatl' language, but his *General History of the Things of New Spain* is a veritable encyclopedia of the Aztec civiliza-tion. He drew it up with a team of literate natives, and he was able to know through his co-workers traditions which are ignored today. His description of native Mexico has lost none of its value and represents a primary and fundamental source for South-American historians of our time."

In the missionary history of Latin America, the question of the "Reductions" (a system of bringing Indians under control), often arose. It is important to note that before being a political or economic system of the regrouping of people, reduction was primarily a method of evangelization. The missionaries were not seeking to Hispanicize the Indians, they were often opposed to the policies of the crown which largely favored the Hispanicization of the Indians. The religious proceeded especially out of a concern to protect their Christians, both from themselves, and against any contact with the bad example of the Spanish. For this double purpose, even before the Jesuits of Brazil as well as those of Paraguay, the friars organized villages from which the Spanish were excluded and where the new converts lived in a practically air-tight chamber. These villages were directed by the missionaries with the help of native chiefs, and they comprised the habitual elements of every human and religious community—church, residence for the religious, school, workshops, residences for the Indians, hospital, and dispensary.

For decades no construction of these Christian villages was undertaken in stone because of the lack of financial means, and the lack of qualified workers. Priority was accorded to health needs and of food-producing work. They were content to build their houses of wood or of mud. This fact explains why we possess no vestiges of the way of life of this period; not even a written document.

The anecdotal history of the missions has kept the name of André Thévet alive. A friar, born at Angouleme in 1502, Thévet visited the Moluccas, Bizerte, and Cairo, and travelled through Italy. Thirsting for knowledge much like Rabelais, whom he met in Rome and with whom he formed a friendship, he studied at Poitiers and at Paris. In 1555 he accompanied the expedition of Durand de Villegagnon to Brazil. After his return he was named chaplain to Catherine de Medici and historian and cosmographer to the king; he died in 1592. Among other works, he wrote, *a Cosmography of the Levant,* and the *Singularities of Antarctic France.* He gave his name to a South American tree, the thevetia. He, among others, played a key role in the discovery and the spread of tobacco, "l'herbe petun," for which he acquired a fondness. He carried some of the seeds back to Europe, planted them in his garden of simple things at Paris, and baptized the petun "herbe angoulmoisine" in honor of his native city.

Let us look at several examples to get an idea of the successes and the vicissitudes of the apostolate in Latin America. In Colombia, in 1550, forty years after the arrival of the Franciscans, there were 200,000 baptized Indians. In Peru, by the end of the sixteenth century, Lima possessed a great friary with two-hundred religious, two colleges and a Franciscan house of recollection. In Venezuela, it is estimated that thirty of the missionaries were martyred during the course of this century.

It is interesting here to point out that the first black to be canonized was a Franciscan—Saint Benedict the Moor. Son of black slaves imported into Sicily, he was born in 1526 at San Filadelphia, later renamed San Fratello in his honor. At the age of twenty-one he entered a small community of hermits of Saint Francis, where he remained for fifteen years. He then became a member of the Observant movement and was successively cook and superior of the friary of Palermo. He accomplished numerous miracles, among them the resuscitation of several dead persons. He died in 1589; his feast is celebrated in the Order each year on April 3.

V.
The Seventeenth Century

In the course of the Great Century, so called because of all the social change, the Protestant Reform, and the religious wars, and the Counter Reform, there were few changes in the structure of the Order. There is scarcely anything to consider on this point except the definitive approval of the Capuchin constitutions, approved by Urban VIII in 1643. The entire Order followed its expansion in practicing the traditional activities of intellectual, missionary, charitable, and social activity.

Intellectual Activity

For Franciscan thought, as in all other areas, the seventeenth century was truly the "Great Century." Intellectual activity itself was stimulated by the Protestant controversy, Jansenism, and Quietism.

First, knowledge and historical research. The Order recognizes and has been ever grateful towards the pioneer of historical research, Friar Luke Wadding (1588-1657). This young Irish Friar, educated at the College of Lisbon and at the University of Coimbra, visited the libraries of Europe, collected manuscripts from the archives of the friaries especially in Italy, and in 1623, obtained for his Order the edition of the *Writings of Saint Francis*. It was to furnish a precious base, the most solid of references, in the effort undertaken to find the original ideal of the founder. In 1639, Wadding published in twelve volumes the *Complete Works* of John Duns Scotus. Between times appeared the tomes of his monumental work, the *Annales* of the Order, which permitted the renewal of historical studies.

Among the representatives of historiography it is necessary to cite especially Arthur de Moustier, author of a very erudite Franciscan *Martyrology*. Jean de la Haye, over the course of twenty-five years, published 40 volumes of his celebrated *Biblia Maxima*, a collection of the best commentaries on the Bible.

Saint Lawrence of Brindisi, a Capuchin, was an exegete and a theologian with a very rich patristic background. Robert de Cambrai, another Capuchin, brought out in 1680 his *Aurifodina Universalis*, an inexhaustible treasury of the citations of authors on all religious subjects. A Conventual, Cardinal Brancati, an eminent Scotist, developed the theses of the Order on the Incarnation and the Kingship of Jesus Christ. The theology of the Immaculate Conception was furthered and made great progress. One of the masters of canon law was Anaclete Reiffenstuel (+1703) whose works would serve as a manual until 1850.

There are some strange and touching examples of the work of the Franciscans in the 17th century. One finds a confused scattering of erudition, including the *General Index* of the writings of Saint Bonaventure brought forth by Friar Barthelemy of Berberis who dedicated his entire life to this work. The complete *General Index* of the writings of St. Bonaventure is still very useful today. Among the works of this century are also found popular songs destined to be sung in the course of parish missions, as well as pure contemplation and light poetry all tied together, as in the *Psalms* of Friar Martial of Brives (+1693). Occult sciences are mixed with theology, as in the works of P. Belin, a Capuchin and the bishop of Belley.

Jansenism and Quietism

The reform of the Abbey of Port Royal had, as its anecdotal origin, the sermon of a travelling Capuchin who preached there in 1608 before Mother Angelique. The sudden conversion, the break with the world, and the famous scene at the grill are part of literary history. It was another Capuchin, a converted Protestant, Archangel de Pembrok, who directed the nuns of Port Royal up to 1622.

Jansenist rigorism which belittled and depreciated human nature all the way to depreciating God, his creation and his redemption, met an equal adversary in the optimistic humanism of the sons of the Saint Francis. The Capuchin, Ives of Paris, especially, attacked the followers of Arnaud and his *Frequent Communion,* in his "Very humble remonstrances to the Queen against the new doctrines of this time."

At the same time, François Faure "refuted" the *Provinciales* of Blaise Pascal, and Zachary of Lisieux wrote his *Journal of a Voyage into the Land of Jansenism,* "where are treated the singularities which are found there, of the customs, manners, and religion of its inhabitants." Timothy of Paris, the secretary of the Procurator of the Order, in Rome, was very active and prepared to condemn the Jansenist Quesnel.

After Jansenism, there was another enemy of the faith—Quietism. Quietism erred not by a lack of confidence and hope, but by the excess of sentiment and emotion. If it did not provoke or bring about the same polemic reaction in the Franciscan ranks, and even if it seemed to appear, wrongly, to have colored the writings of this or that author (as for example, Benedict of Canfield or Lawrence of Paris), Quietism was for the spiritual authors of the seventeenth century the occasion of a demonstration of sanctity in their writing on the highest mysticism. Claude Frassen, guardian of Paris; Joseph de Tremblay, the Grey Eminence; Yves of Paris, untiring writer, always solid and sure of himself; Paul de Lagny; Alexander de la Ciotat; and many others knew how to speak of the prayer of contemplation without confusing it with a morbid abandon and without disassociating it from other means and expressions, wished by God, for the whole spiritual life. In reference to Benedict of Canfield, Bremond writes: "Of all the influences which have fashioned the prayer life of the 17th century, there is not one which surpasses him." As to Lawrence of Paris, when he died at the Friary of Meudon, the 12th of April, 1631, he left two enormous volumes: *TheTapestries of Divine Love,* and *The Palace of Divine Love,* (appearing in 1602); these were the first mystical works of the seventeenth century.

But practice was on a par with theory. The hermitages, a tradition within the Order, continued to receive the support of the friars. Still new ones were being established, for example, in 1660, at La Ferte-Alais.

Saint Francis and Bossuet

In order to better appreciate the Franciscan impact upon the "Great Century," one can read what Saint Francis and the Franciscan movement inspired in the wise and learned Bossuet. Here is the beginning of a panegyric on the Poverello by Bossuet, the Bishop of Meaux, to the friars and their friends and benefactors gathered to celebrate the feast of St. Francis.

"What do you think, my Reverend Fathers, I wish to do today from this sacred pulpit? You have assembled your friends and illustrious benefactors for them to pay their respects to your holy patriarch, and I pretend nothing more than to pass for a madman for I only wish to recall his foolishness. David knew that there was a sublime and heavenly foolishness; it is this divine madness that Saint Francis possessed.

"God, in his first work, had created everything with wisdom, measure, and proportion; in the second place, reparation through the folly of the Cross; he did not know any moderation; he only advanced more and more with his foolish steps; he leaped over the mountains and the hills, from heaven to the Crib, from the Crib to the Cross, from the Cross to the tomb and to the depths of hell, and from there to the heights of heaven. Everything is without order, everything is without measure. By the same process that the infinite is joined to our finiteness, by the same process the finite is elevated to the infinite and is lost in the infinite and this loss in the infinite seems to be a miscarriage or a deviation. Such is the foolishness of Francis.

"Do you see this, Christians, this Francis, this rich merchant of Assisi, whose father sends him to Rome for the affairs of business, do you see him who talks and converses with a poor man in the middle of the street? Oh, God!—what does a businessman have in common with this type of person? What business or transaction does he wish to have with this poor man that for his clothes, he gives him his own? Afterwards, overcome by such a beautiful exchange, he seems to be completely joyful in clothes of rags, as much as the poor man can scarcely recognize himself in the clothes of a wealthy person. Ah!—how he begins to understand the profession of the madness of the Cross."

Here, presented in the century of the Sun King, by one of his most illustrious orators, is the person and the spirituality of the one who is called: "the most ardent, the most transported, and if I dare to speak in this manner, the most desperate lover of poverty who has ever existed in the Church."

Means of Action

Books were not the only arms used in the battle against Jansenism and Quietism. They would have been insufficient. All kinds of methods and means of action were utilized and in every possible area. Based on the chronicles and memoirs of the time, it was the Capuchins and the Recollects who exercised an influence, similar to that of the clergy, monks, and canons in daily life of the Middle Ages, with perhaps the same factor of picturesqueness and of sympathy. Unfortunately, though, the friars were sometimes made the object of caricature.

Jean-Pierre Camus, bishop and novelist, distinguished himself in this area by his realistic, tough, and earthy zest. He styled the mendicants as "jugs who lower themselves in order to fill themselves up better," an allusion to the capuche which held the alms received from the faithful. "Jesus Christ," he said, "with only five loaves of bread and two fish was able to nourish three thousand people, and that, only once in his lifetime. Saint Francis, with several habited followers is able to nourish 40,000 do-nothings, as if by a miracle." To the attack of Camus, Father Yves of Paris, replied in a beautiful apology of the religious life in his *Happy Success of Piety,* or "The Triumph of Religious Life over the World and Heresy."

The importance of the individual apostolate was also felt in this century where spiritual direction became a mode of life for the members of the nobility and the middle-class. A certain "illuminism," which held that the soul only trust itself for the truths of the Cross and the conduct of the Christian life, made spiritual direction for many an important part of life. The Friars Minor did not refuse to break the bread of doctrine and the bread of mysticism for those starved souls who asked for direction. Benedict of Canfield directed Madame Acarie (Blessed Marie of the Incarnation).

Father Cyprian of Gamaches directed Queen Henriette of England. President Lamoignon had in his garden at Baville a hermitage reserved for a Franciscan.

The friars participated also in the daily life of the time, even to the material cares of their contemporaries, and especially the poor. The Capuchins were among the first firemen of Paris. It was also during this period that the "Mountains of Piety" developed further. The "Mountains of Piety" begun by Bernardine of Feltre several centuries earlier, in order to fight against usury, loaned money to the poor at a very low rate of interest, and were similar to savings and loan banks. Numerous examples of modern banks in Italy are still called "Montes Pietatis." Care of and visiting the sick absorbed much of the time and the devotion of the friars. In 1668, after one of the decrees of Parliament, it was realized that two-hundred and sixty-eight Capuchins had died in the course of the preceding years, victims of their care of the sick during the epidemic.

Along with social activity, many religious were also involved in political activity. There is a Lars Skytte, Swedish diplomat, head of a mission to Denmark, Germany, and Holland, and finally to Lisbon, where he converted. He became a friar in 1647 under the name of Friar Lawrence of Saint-Paul. He was the confessor to Queen Christina of Sweden beginning in 1668 and author of *Voyages to the Holy Places,* which could be better entitled, "Memories of my Conversion." There is Joseph du Tremblay who had great influence over Cardinal Richelieu. Saint Lawrence of Brindisi led the Crusade against the Turks and also worked for peace between Bavaria and Spain and between Savoy and Mantua. Mark of Aviano was the chaplain for the soldiers of Jan Sobiewski of Poland in 1683. Capuchins and Recollects, through their simple spirit and open frankness, fulfilled the role of military chaplains and attracted the attention of Louis xiv where he admired them at the siege of La Rochelle.

They filled their role of being chaplains admirably all through the Thirty Years War, 1618-1648.

But the most popular ministries of the Order were still the traditional apostolates of the Third Order and the missions.

The founding of the fraternities of the Third Order were the means of favoring spiritual progress among the faithful, the formation of a religious laity, and a means of helping to spread the evangelical ideals. The First Order increased its influence through the support of many such fraternities. Madrid, in 1685, had 25,000 tertiaries. In Italy, the foundation and the upkeep of many charitable activities was due to the work of the tertiaries: hospitals, orphanages, and soup kitchens. In France, the influence of the Third Order was felt in the area of religious life in the formation of congregations such as the Congregation of the Most Blessed Sacrament.

Preaching remained the daily work. The printed lists of sermons and panegyrics of the seventeenth century, numerous and rather pompous, should not hide the true character of Franciscan preaching. The most beautiful sermons and those which had the greatest impact were probably never printed.

Parish missions were one of the favored ministries. They were, at one and the same time a retreat, a session of formation, a catechism of perserverance, a battle against indifference, heresy, and atheism. These missions began on Sunday afternoon after vespers, and continued for five to six weeks.

"Each day," writes twentieth century Italian friar Agostino Gemelli, "the missionaries gave the people instructions, meditations, dialogue conferences, and catechism lessons intermingled with prayers and songs. There were processions and distributions of books of piety ... The missions attracted great crowds. Almost always they brought

about happy results, such as reconciliation between ene-
mies, return of stolen objects, help given to the poor, the beginnings of fraternities. Above all else, they reeducated the
conscience of the people . . . ." Even a Father Honorius de
Camus, despite his verbal eccentricities, touched the hearts
of people and converted them. The Capuchin, Seraphin of
Paris was celebrated by La Bruyere as the ideal preacher,
"the court deserted the royal chapel of Versailles and went
to mingle with the people in order to listen to him."

The Counter Reform

Some of the parish missions were very specialized in
the struggle against Protestantism. One example will illus-
trate in what climate they sometimes took place. A decree
of Monsieur l' Intendant of Bourgogne is still kept at the
National Library in Paris. Obtained by Father Duhan, a friar
and guardian of the friary at Vezelay, the decree was against
several of the so-called reformed religious who wished to
kill him. Here are the facts.

Father Duhan, a former Protestant minister, went in
1667 with one of his confreres, Father Robineau and two
Capuchins, to Vault-de-Lugny, near Avallon. They had been
invited by the owner of the castle, Madame d' Ausson to
participate in a Protestant synod, (gathering of clergy to
discuss issues). There were more than four thousand in the
audience. The synod was to last for five days. At the beginning, the discussions went well; but on the last day it was
learned that a Pastor Dolon had sworn to kill Father Duhan.
To prepare for this, he had hidden, twenty guns in one house
and forty in another house. On the final day, the public
debate had scarcely begun when an armed party inter-
rupted it. Forty members of the audience were wounded,
among them the superior of the College of Avallon and a

canon. Pastor Dolon wounded an attorney of the king with several sword blows and then threw himself upon Father Duhan, but the supporters of Father Duhan disengaged him. "Providence," says the Chronicle, "saw to it that the guns intended for Father Duhan did not work." The only gun which worked was used by the first cousin of Father Duhan, but the bullet missed its mark. Thus ended another incident in the battle between the Catholics and Protestants without anyone's being killed.

Foreign Missions

A new persecution in Japan added forty-five Franciscans to the list of martyrs and closed the country to Europeans for two more centuries. But the seed had been solidly planted. Two centuries later, when Japan reopened its door, Father Petitjean, who disembarked in 1865, received a visit from a dozen of the descendants of the Catholics of the seventeenth century. A little later, ten-thousand secret Catholics made themselves known. Baptism and the faith had been handed down from one generation to the next. They had kept the name of Saint Francis in the *Confiteor* of the Mass, a reminder of the formulas of the Third Order which had been so flourishing two centuries before.

Other conquests compensated for the loss of Japan at that time. In Turkey, a mission of the Capuchins which had been sent by Cardinal Richelieu landed in Constantinople.

Saint Francis Solano having landed in Peru, travelled through Chaco for some years with his portable altar and his violin with which he occasionally accompanied the songs and the Psalms. When he died in 1610, the viceroy and the archbishop of Lima themselves carried the remains of this humble friar. His feast day is July 14.

For the Recollect Friars the whole of Canada was an

ideal field for them to plant the Cross. They accepted the invitation of Champlain and came to establish themselves on the banks of the Saint Lawrence, in the Province of Quebec. Father Denis Jamet celebrated the first Mass in Canada on an island near Montreal on the 24th of June, 1615. The following year the Huron Missions were founded. In 1625 Father Nicholas Viel was martyred, and in 1629 Quebec fell into the hands of the English who drove the missionaries out. It would be necessary to wait forty more years before the Recollects were able to return to New France. In 1763 the treaty of Paris definitively gave Canada to the English, and this was the formal end of the mission.

Within the context of Canadian history the friars contributed to the development of the major art movement, the Beaux-Arts. A Recollect, Claude François, in religion Brother Luc (1615-1685), was a renowned painter and a student of LeBrun. Originally from Amiens, François studied at Rome where he knew Poussin and Claude Lorrain. Subsequently he entered the Recollects and worked in the friaries of Paris, Saint Germain-en-Laye, Chalons-sur-Marne, and Amiens. In the spring of 1670 he embarked with six other friars who established the Recollects once again in Quebec. Eventually he returned to France and using his talents decorated the chapel of the friary of Sezanne (Marne), with vignettes from the life of Saint Francis. It is now the public hospital.

Father Louis Hennepin, a Franciscan, accompanied the expedition of LaSalle to Niagara. The French missionaries also accompanied the first discoverers of Australia in 1606. These new extensions made up for several setbacks in Africa. The Franciscan missions of Morocco, of the Congo, and of Ethiopia only met with persecution. By the end of the century, in the Holy Land, only the sanctuaries of Bethlehem and the Holy Sepulchre were recovered for the friars. There had been disagreements not only among the various rites, but even among the friars themselves.

VI.
The Eighteenth Century

The eighteenth century was a time of trials and of decline for the Franciscan Order, as well as for other religious orders. For the first part of the century, the friars were flourishing. Towards the middle of the century the First Order numbered 40,000 Observants, 19,000 Reformed, 11,000 Recollects, 7,000 Discalced, altogether 77,000 religious spread among 4,050 houses, and approximately 6,200 Capuchins in 430 houses. Numerous and active, they are found in every area of study, preaching, and in works of charity—at Marseille, for example, during the Plague of 1720, fifty-seven friars caring for the plague stricken died. The Order was also a victim of the War of the Spanish Succession (1701-1713), as well as of the wave of atheism and deism which spread over Europe. It was also caught in the wave of anti-Roman nationalism which took the political names of Gallicanism or Josephism, and to close the century, the Order became the victim of revolutionary persecutions as well.

Free Thought

It was only natural that in the name of "liberty" and "freedom" from superstition the attacks of the sixteenth century against the religious vows were taken up again. It was logical too in the age of the Enlightenment, that in order to wipe out so-called ignorance and superstition, efforts were made to eliminate the Order whose influence over the masses was enormous, and whose "fanaticism" prevented "Reason" from reaching the people. The Franciscan Order thus had the honor of serving as the target of mockery or the calumny of Bayle in his *Dictionary,* and of Knight Jaucourt in his *Encyclopedia.* Among the pamphlets of Voltaire, one can find examples of the ridicule of the friars.

The tactic of the hostile war was coldly elaborated. D'Alembert expressly said, "We will praise the Franciscans in the article of the 'Cordeliers,' but we can look again at them in the article 'Capuchons' where we can poke fun at them and ridicule them."

Even such a writer as Le Sage is not able to prevent himself in his *Bachelier de Salamanque* from describing as very lax, the life in the friaries of Mexico, their banquets, their card parties, and giving to understand that this was a universal fact.

Parallel to the cold war, open ridicule was also undertaken. A book of Poullin de Lumina (sometimes attributed to d'Alembert) already states in its title the general program, *The History of the Mendicant Monks, where the very rapid progress of the two Orders is treated, (Minors and Preachers), of the laxity that has occurred in their discipline, and of the troubles which they have brought on both the Church and the State.* The work appeared in Avignon in 1767.

The following year, there appeared in the *Acta Sanctorum* the monumental study on the Franciscan sources of the Bollandist Suyskens. The text available up to that point was an unedited manuscript of the "First Life of Saint Francis" by Thomas of Celano (written in 1228), as well as the "Legend of the Three Companions." But the so-called century of history held on to its passion rather than to its solid documents.

In order to fight against this hostile current it would have been necessary that there be a firm direction, an organization, and counsels universally received and accepted. But during the entire first quarter of the century events in Europe prevented the ministers general from holding a chapter, a situation which continued until 1768 for other reasons as well.

It would have been necessary also to have strong temperaments and dedicated capable writers. The only polemicist of value was Jean-Nicholas-Hubert Hayer, born at Sarrelouis in France in 1708. Hayer, a professor of theology of the province of Saint Denis, was a renowned spiritual author who founded, in 1757, a review entitled, *Religion Avenged, or a Refutation of Impious Authors by a Society of Men of Letters.*"

Moreover, the common people were less influenced by printed arguments than by certain accounts and anecdotes, authentic or not, which provided topics of conversations for long evenings in thatched cottages. Here is an example. A philosophe (learned man, or philosopher) on a journey came across a Capuchin on foot in the snow and cried out to him, "You there, Capuchin, acknowledge that if God does not exist, you are a proud imbecile!" And the Capuchin replied, "You there, philosophe, if God exists, acknowledge that you are proudly more stupid than I am."

Despite all these warring efforts, research in the Order was valiantly carried on. Parallel with the study already referred to since the *Acta Sanctorum,* the Friars Minor began to collect the documents and the sources of their history in two fundamental works—the second edition and the continuation of the *Annales* of Luke Wadding by Father Sbaralea. Thus, the essential testimonies will be preserved before the dispersion and the secularization of the friaries, which caused the loss of many archives. These scientific works will allow the Franciscan family to take up the study of itself again at a later period.

In the disciplines other than history, we must point out the work of Ferraris in canon law. In spirituality, the work of

Ambrose de Lombez, the author of a renowned *Treatise on Interior Peace* which went through sixty editions in France alone. Bernardine Clifton, of the friary of the English Franciscans at Douai, wrote a vigorous defense of the papal bull *"Unigenitus"* which brought persecution on him as well as on his confreres from the Jansenist bishops.

But all this was a somewhat futile action. Neither the renewal of interest in the contemplative life with the houses of retreat founded by Blessed Bonaventure of Barcelona at Rome or the houses founded by Saint Theophilus of Corte, nor the successes of traditional preaching with such giants as Saint Leonard of Port Maurice could prevent the decline of the Order. The little books of the door-to-door salesmen innoculated the middle class with an anti-clerical virus which would become difficult to eliminate.

Gallicanism

Political Gallicanism (French independence, or freedom from Rome) had already, in the preceding century, inspired the conduct of Louis xiv against the Order and now intensified its attacks in the course of the 18th century. This was not a phenomenon peculiar to France alone, for it can be found in all of Europe wherever the theories of Josephism found their way. The civil authority intervened in all religious affairs, wishing to dispose of the goods of the Church, as well as of religious persons, and to attach to itself the right of intervening in every case between Rome and the citizen of each state.

When the king in 1751, on the basis of a report of the count of Noailles concerning a Recollect of Versailles, forbade shoes of wood and prescribed leather shoes, this was only a puerile detail. An edict of 1768 fixing the minimum age for vows at twenty-one years for men and eighteen for women was acceptable, but other interventions exceeding the civil competence were veritable infringements. For example, the transfer of friaries from the Recollects to the Cordeliers, the limitations of the number of houses for each order and of the number of novices admitted, and the forbidding of French capitulars of participating in the general chapters of the Order. From 1768 to 1830 the friars were not able to convoke or hold a general chapter. It was thus impossible to elect a minister general during all this time and it was the Holy See who appointed the holders of this position.

If Joseph, the Hapsburg emperor of Austria-Hungary, is called the "Sacristan-King" because he regulated the ceremonies of the liturgy, what is to be said of the king of France who wished to regulate even the consciences of his subjects? "His Majesty is informed that there are several abuses to foresee or to root out on the subject of cases whose absolution is reserved to superiors, and also that the transfers (changes of residence) are too frequent and without legitimate cause and are tiring out the religious . . . ."

Under the pretext of reform, it was the dissolution of the orders that the Commission of Regulars aimed at. Instituted in 1766, the Commission of Regulars was composed in large part of laymen and four prelates but not a single religious. The head of the commission was Lomenie de Brienne, the archbishop of Toulouse. It is true that Gallicanism had its supporters in positions of authority. For example, the chapter of the province of Saint Denis in 1752 ruled to submit itself in everything to His Majesty because the minister general of the Order wrote that it was necessary to obey one's Sovereign in everything. Instead of repulsing them, the chapter solicited the interventions of princes; and finally, even of twenty-seven Masonic Lodges, most of them had as their head regular clergy . . . .

To cut off a religious order from Rome is to try to cut a tree off from its roots. Decline is not far away, even if it is only temporary. With its train of failures, of sorrowful interrogations, of quarrels, and infidelities, even before undergoing the blows of the Revolution, the Order had received trials from which it would be difficult to recover.

The Great Revolution

Decline was thus continuing. But those who during the quarter of a century preceding the French Revolution had, despite everything, resisted the decay and the rotting, found the strength to be martyrs in the end.

The scaffold in France and the various executions found more than two-hundred victims in the three branches of the First Order. Among others, John Francis Burté, Apollinaris Morel, and Séverin Girault, martyred in 1792 at the Carmelite Friary in Paris, are now celebrated as Blesseds on September 2 of each year. On the prison ships of Nantes, in 1794, ten perished by drowning and about fifty perished in the prison ships of Rochefort.

One can only deplore several spectacular defections, that of Eulogius Schneider, for example. This German writer became a Recollect in 1788. He was well known as a preacher at Stuttgart, then as a professor of philosophy at Augsburg. He left the Order and became a French politician. Taking the constitutional oath at Strasbourg in 1791, he became mayor of Hagenau, a Jacobin deputy, public accuser, and was responsible for bringing the reign of terror to Alsace. He ended up by being guillotined at Paris in 1794.

On the 13th of February 1790, the constitution forbade the taking of vows, abolished the religious orders, and all religious were banished or dispersed. "After a more or less long wait," writes Pierre de La Gorce, "the religious learned by means of notification in which monasteries they should be gathered together. Like soldiers with their marching be gathered together. Like soldiers with their marching orders, they took to the roads towards their new destinations. They left without complaining, with hardly any good-byes . . . . In each department (state), two or three houses received those who had remained faithful religious."

Searches and inventories were conducted with a beating of drums; and in Italy, the armies of the first consul, Napoleon, gave themselves over to pillage. Throughout the entire territory of Napoleon's empire, the Order was ravaged, almost annihilated, reduced to several clandestine fraternities. Around 1815 the Order would only number 14,000 religious, living primarily in Spain and in America. And during the following century, Spain itself would see in thirty years (1832-1862) a loss of friars from 9,000 to230.

The Missions

Even in China and the Holy Land, the friars knew persecution. In China, when persecution should have brought about a spirit of unity and cooperation in all efforts, an internal controversy arose which was a crowning misfortune and most prejudicial to the work of the missions: the quarrel over rites. Among the usages and customs and ceremonies of the Chinese people, many had value and significance only as civil and profane customs. They were indifferent as concerns religion, so the Christians tried to continue the practice of them.

On the other hand, certain rites were more intimately tied to cult, such as ceremonies in honor of Confucius. Were the Christians permitted to adopt them? The Jesuits asserted yes; the majority of the Franciscans said no. The quarrel became acrimonious and even brought on scandal. It only ended when Benedict XIV condemned the rites in question. Unfortunately, this was a total and brutal rejection which brought to naught all efforts at assimilation and integration.

In North America, Texas was fertile missionary land, primarily the apostolate of the celebrated friar Antonio Margil (+1762). The most beautiful masterpiece of missionary activity in the New World was the chain of missions established by the Franciscans in California. This territory was entrusted to the care of the friars in 1767 and the principal merit for the string of missions belongs to a missionary of exceptional toughness, Junipero Serra (1713-1784), originally from Majorca, beatified by Pope John Paul II on Sept. 25, 1988. He organized the foundation of the missions which became flourishing and happy centers of "Reduction" and which later became the nuclei of the great cities of California. It is fascinating to point out that San Francisco, settled on the 17th of September, 1776, (the Feast of the Stigmata of Saint Francis), still recalls today the memory of the Poverello with its very name.

Los Angeles is named after the Portiuncola chapel, the chapel of Our Lady of the Angels, the church repaired by Francis himself. Also, the original name of Santa Fe is, "The Royal City of the Holy Faith of Blessed Francis."

VII.
The Nineteenth Century

The nineteenth century began with most religious orders at the lowest point of their existence. The disastrous effects of the French Revolution and the suppression of most religious communities throughout the countries of Europe did not augur well for the the future of religious life. Anti-Catholic, anti-religious, and anti-clerical feelings were rampant throughout the continent.

For the Church of France, the nineteenth century opened with the Concordat of 1801. Among its other curiosities, this ageement between France and the Vatican did not even mention the regular clergy. A decree of 1804 reduced religious orders to dependence upon the authorization of the government. In 1809, the missionary societies were suppressed; in 1810, the Sulpicians; and in 1811 the Trappists. Even in the occupied or annexed countries, Napoleon ordered the "suppression without distinction of all the monasteries."

This anti-Catholic and anti-clerical feeling flared up again in the Revolution of 1830. Beneath all of this, there were religious who kept trying to live their religious life, and to undertake the apostolate of preaching to the people. Joseph de Maistre has written of this period: "The religious spirit is not yet extinguished in France. It rises up on the mountains, and there it works miracles."

The second half of the century saw the beginnings of a religious revival in the sense of all the religious orders beginning to make a recovery from the devastating effects of the last hundred years, the years of revolutions, and the effects of the Enlightenment. The Franciscan Order as well as other religious orders made a new beginning and enjoyed a rebirth and the opportunity to begin again with renewed ideals.

Rediscovery of Saint Francis

The Romantic Movement, especially in its literary and historical forms, with its return to the glory of the Middle Ages, was especially attracted to the person of Saint Francis. The renewal of interest in the Middle Ages, did not really discover the true and authentic Saint Francis, but it helped prepare the way and in the process made Francis and Franciscan ideals particularly attractive.

In 1826, Joseph Gorres, a romantic, and a converted German nationalist published, *Saint Francis of Assisi, a Troubadour.* This work had wide repercussions, even beyond the German borders. Once the impulse was started, poetry and mysticism entered by the same door into the hagiographical method (study of the saints), holding each other by the hand. Chateaubriand, Michelet, Montalembert, each invoked in turn the charm of the Poverello and of the first generation Franciscans. Chateaubriand wrote in his *Memoires d"Outre Tombe,* "I have received from my patron saint, poverty, love of little ones and humble people, and a compassion for animals." He added, "When the hour will come, it is to the Portinuncola," that he will go, "to ask for solitude."

Taine, in his *Voyage to Italy* avowed his own spirit being dazzled. Ozanam gave to France the *Fioretti* and "The Canticle of Brother Sun." He saw in Francis the "Orpheus of the Middle Ages." Liszt composed in music "The Sermon to the Birds." Renan described Umbria as the "Italian Galilee." Anatole France was overcome by the charm of Franciscan

Assisi. "Gentle" and "exquisite" are the epithets which most often come from the pens of these authors.

Almost as often these authors used the words, "revolutionary" and "rebel." That is why though romantic, the century with its illusions of rationalist pretensions as well as its anticlerical feelings, took pleasure in setting Francis against the pope, the prophet against the priest, initiative against obedience. Certain ones denied the Stigmata, and many made Francis out to be the first Protestant, the champion of individual liberties. Renan, in spite of his own assertion that "Francis was truly a second Christ," nevertheless presents Francis as rebellious or insubordinate in his break with the theocracy of Innocent III.

After the outbreak of sympathy—powerful yet confused and unmethodical—true historical research had its hour when Paul Sabatier, in 1894 published his *Life of Saint Francis*. This work has been translated and read throughout the entire world. Sabatier is truly the initiator of modern studies on Saint Francis. Solidity and documentation, a finesse of psychological analysis, clarity and emotion, and an evocative style makes his work great. Nevertheless an underlying theme clouds the perspective, namely, that of the thesis of the confiscation of the evangelical Franciscan movement from the beginnings to the profit of a pretended Vatican domination. One sentence of his "Introduction" calls to mind the thesis, "If the thirteenth century is par excellence, the century of saints, it is also the century of heretics; we will see that these two words are not as contradictory as they seem to be."

Without Sabatier, however, there would never have been as many historians of quality who turned their attention to The Franciscan Question. The origin, date, value, and reciprocal influence of the sources, and this other question, less theoretical but always a burning issue—the place of Saint Francis in the Church of his time: revolt or submission, liberty or obedience, was a burning question.

Restoration and Activities of the Order

Saint Francis was in fashion for the nineteenth century but not yet for the Franciscans themselves. In Spain and Portugal, proclerical and anti-clerical governments succeeded each other in power. In France, Martignac, in 1828, withdrew from the religious orders the right to teach. Napoleon III was more favorable to the orders, but a decree of Jules Ferry in 1880 forced the orders to ask for legal authorization; this was renewed in a law of 1901. In Germany the "Kulturkampf" conducted warfare against the Church and many of the religious followed the immigrants to the United States, laying the foundations for some of the Amercan provinces of the First Order.

With the various waves of immigrants during this period, members of the various orders and congregations of both men and women came with the immigrants to minister to them in the New World setting. Some of the first American provinces of the friars were established as a result of their growing numbers. The Saint Louis-Chicago Province of the Sacred Heart was established as the first American province of the Friars Minor in the United States in 1879. Many of its members were from Germany and had fled the Kulturkampf. The Province of Saint John the Baptist of Cincinnati, with its roots in Austria, was established in 1886. The New York Province of the Holy Name of Jesus was formally erected in 1901. The Italian Province of New York of the Immaculate Conception was erected in 1910. The Province of the Sacred Heart had been entrusted with the remnants of the California Missions, until in 1915 the California Province of Santa Barbara was formally established. Friars coming with the Polish immigrants during the first part of the century had grown to a sufficient number to become the Province of the Assumption of Pulaski, Wisconsin in 1919. In 1985, the friars of Saint John the Baptist Province working among the Indians and the Spanish-speaking of the Southwest were formally established as the Province of Our Lady of Guadalupe.

Despite all the obstacles in their path, all the orders, including the Franciscans, began to develop once again in Europe. The total number of religious men in France toward the middle of the century rises from three thousand to thirty thousand. The Concordats worked out between the Holy See and the various governments limited somewhat the arbitrariness of these governments. Charitable and missionary activity were undertaken without persecution.

Everywhere in the world, the Third Order, which Leo XIII publicly praised, enjoyed new beginnings. Many bishops and priests, among others the Cure of Ars, honored it by becoming tertiaries. "The Third Order demonstrated the living gospel," says Pope Leo XIII and, "awoke the spirit of love of faith and of peace shining in the thirteenth century with Saint Francis as a true sun."

At the seventh centenary of the birth of Francis in 1882, numerous writings and speeches celebrated the civilizing action of the Franciscan movement of the nineteenth century. Francis had been re-discovered esthetically by the artists, intellectually by the men of studies, and popularly by the men and women who witnessed the activity of his sons and daughters. Louis Veuillot was able to write, "The future belongs to the barefooted ones."

The intellectual activity of the Order showed new signs of life. At Quaracchi, near Florence, the *Complete Works* of Saint Bonaventure were published in a critical edition. Two astonishing numbers were behind the work: the editors visited four hundred libraries and examined more than fifty thousand manuscripts.

Franciscan history in Italy owed much to a brilliant and solid precursor, Father Nicholas Papini, who had brought forth at Foligno, even before Paul Sabatier, his *History of Francis of Assisi.* Written in 1825, it had a revealing subtitle, "Critical Works." But the time was not yet ripe. Political events were unfavorable, literary criticism still in its cradle, and hence the work did not receive the publicity or popularity that it merited. It was in 1885 that the edition of the *Sources* appeared in the first volume of *Analecta Franciscana* at Quaracchi. Numerous important texts from Franciscan History were now published, such as *The Second Life of Saint Francis* by Thomas of Celano, or the *Chronicles* of Jordan of Giano, of Salimbene, of Eccleston, and even the *Complete Works* of John Duns Scotus.

In order to continue this effort, societies and international reviews on the grand scale were established towards the end of the century and at the beginning of the twentieth century. The majority of these still exist today and continue their brilliant scientific career.

Much more humble, and ephemeral as well, but efficacious and adapted to the time was the foundation of the Franciscan minor seminaries. After the first one was founded in 1869, the provinces of the Order emphasized this instrument of formation and of recruitment which furnished hundreds of vocations for the Order. The majority of these young men in the seminaries would never have been able to receive the education that was provided for them in the minor seminaries. Various causes have led today to the disappearance of the majority of these schools, but the number of religious who were formed in them gives witness to the dedication of the men who taught in the schools. The minor Franciscan seminaries still actually enroll seventy-five hundred students today.

The Missions

The Franciscan missionary epic likewise continued in this century of colonizers. Certain missions underwent an eclipse, but elsewhere, traditional apostolates were valiantly maintained. Schools, dispensaries, social foundations to fight slavery or famine, and the building of churches were all undertaken. The work of the Franciscan missions as well as that of the Church remains both a civilization action and an evangelizing mission.

The Friars Minor knew persecution in many places: in Mexico in 1816 and 1834, in Bolivia in 1810, in the Holy Land in 1860 with the martyrs of Damascus massacred by the Druses. In the *Journey from Paris to Jerusalem* of Chateaubriand, one can read about the numberless vexations to which the friars had to submit. Nevertheless, the friars returned to Egypt in 1839, to Argentina in 1855, to Morocco in 1858. Flourishing missions were organized in the Philippines and numbered more than 1.2 million Christians. The Capuchins went to Ethiopia and to Egypt in 1846, to Chili in 1848, and to Brazil along the Atlantic coast in 1860; the evangelization of the Indians of the Amazon was entrusted to the Franciscans. The same year, 1834, when the Spanish Franciscans were exiled from Mexico, Andre Herrero returned to Bolivia with twelve Italian Franciscans and the following year he brought a new band of eighty-three missionaries which permitted the reopening or the founding of missions in Chili and Peru.

Missionaries became more and more ethnologists and linguists. Father Cosi composed a Chinese dictionary; Father Giannecchini of Bolivia composed a Chiriguano Catechism. In Peru, Father Plaza, after fifty years in the mission was justly celebrated for his knowledge of many Indian dialects.

Part of the mission activity in the nineteenth century

was the expansion of the womens' missionary congregations which helped to add to the numerous institutes, hospitals, and schools already existing. It would be necessary to go back to the Middle Ages in order to find the example of religious institutes expanding with such suddenness and such vigor: the Franciscan Missionaries of Egypt; the Franciscans of the Sacred Heart—who endeavored to work especially in America among the immigrants; the Franciscans of the Propagation of the Faith—especially in Morocco and in Central Africa; the Franciscans of Calais—in Ethiopia, Somalia, and now in Togo; the Franciscans of Our Lady of the Angels—in the missions in India.

One of the more important of the female missionary congregations which had its birth during this period was the Institute of the Franciscan Missionaries of Mary, founded in 1877. The foundress, Helen de Chappotin de Neuville, in religion, Mother Marie of the Passion, collaborated for some years with the Jesuits in India. The first community was begun near Madras; then a novitiate was opened in France at Saint-Brieuc. In 1852, Father Bernardine, then minister general of the Friars Minor, received the profession of all the sisters and attached the new Institute to the Third Order Regular. After a short time, this institute received its consecration in blood. When the Boxer Rebellion broke out in 1900, seven of the religious were martyred, a deed which provided a new missionary impulse for the institute which today numbers approximately nine thousand religious, half of whom are non-European. There are eight-hundred and fifty houses of the Institute, two hundred and fifty of which are in Asia.

VIII.
Twentieth Century:
Evolution and Statistics

Finally, we arrive at the twentieth century. As with all other religious institutes, the Franciscan Order suffered from the two World Wars, as much in its numbers as in its activities. Principally in Europe the loss was great: deaths in combat, prisoners of war, civil victims of bombardments, prisoners in concentration camps. Among the prisoners in the concentration camps there were many friars from various nations. Perhaps the best known of them is Father Maximillian Kolbe, now Saint Maximillian Kolbe, No. 16670 in the camp at Auschwitz, who sacrificed his life for one of his companions in detention on Aug. 14, 1942. Europe, in 1912, with 14,223 Friars Minor out of the total 16,811 for the entire Order, represented 85.3% of the whole, constituting more than two thirds of the entire Order.

While the European provinces were suffering a decline in numbers, those in America began in flourish, as did American Franciscanism. A variety of apostolates including parishes, missionary activities, educational institutions, in short, all areas of pastoral activity blossomed. Canadian Franciscans made great missionary strides in Korea, Japan and Peru. One of the marks of Franciscanism in Canada is the presence of flourishing fraternities of Secular Franciscans.

As much as from the wars, the Order suffered in various countries from anti-clerical feelings, which from the beginning of the century had been marked by the continuing battle against religious. In France, the Parliament voted in the law of 1901 which subjected all religious congregations and orders to the obligation of governmental authorization and which gave the government the right to dissolve them by decree. Prime Minister Combes rejected systematically every request for official authorization. In 1904 the government forbade religious the right to teach. In 1924 again, the Herriot government wanted to give more force to the laws forbidding congregations. As a result the religious now organized themselves into a League of Defense of Religious Veterans (le DRAC), and in fighting for their rights, stopped the governmental offensive.

The Seventh Centenary

An auspicious year for Franciscan History was 1926. The celebration of the seventh centenary of the death of Saint Francis gave rise to the blossoming of new interest in Francis and the history of the Order, and for all expressions of Franciscan life. Revues, works of art, expositions, discourses, and theses demonstrated and at the same time stimulated this vitality, bringing thereby a new flourishing of vocations. A cycle of conferences, held at the Sorbonne in Paris, studied in every possible area the influence of Saint Francis on Italian civilization. Even among those who did not belong to any of the three Orders but who called themselves Franciscanists, many great men in art and in thought, voluntarily took part in this praise to honor the Poverello. Among the great names of the French were Edward Jordan, Henri LeMaitre, Etienne Gilson, Edward Schneider, Alexander Masseron, the priest-poet Louis Le Cardonnel, Georges Goyau, Louis Brehier, Louis Gillet, Henri Focillon and many others. There was even an essay on the Protestant Third Order by W. Monod.

François Mauriac in his *Actualite' de Saint Francois,* established a striking parallel between two great mystics, each influential in his own century. "What Saint Francis did in his century, Mahatma Ghandi will accomplish in ours. There is often talk of Christian truths becoming foolish yet the world still runs after them. As if the truth of Christ had not been foolish from the beginning: and in particular what he taught on the mountain—blessed are the gentle. Chased away from the Christian West, this gentleness has found its asylum among the idols and found a dwelling place in the heart of that indomitable skeleton, Ghandi."

The Missions

The 19th century was called the missionary century because of the widespread preaching of the gospel in all areas of the world. But the twentieth century saw the establishment of stable autonomous communities, aided and supported by the older Christian countries. Pius x and Pius xi were the directors and inspirers of this evolution which became more important as the process of decolonization and rise of political independence rendered the missionary process somewhat paternalistic.

Several events are characteristic landmarks that stand out in this process of evolution. In 1926, Pius xi consecrated the first six Chinese bishops, of whom two were Franciscans. Morocco had its first Franciscan priest in 1933. Christian Arab families of Palestine continued to be a source of vocations for the Order. Most of the parishes in the Holy Land entrusted to the friars have beautiful liturgies in the Arab language. Vietnam, which welcomed the return of the friars in 1929 after a long absence, had by 1980 more than a hundred native friars who helped the young province to survive and increase after long and difficult times, and despite the fact that political conditions are so unfavorable to religion.

In the process of missionary efforts, the Bible is being utilized more and more. Two recent translations are remarkable. One is moving because of its text and its illustrations: the Gospel Book and the Catechism in the Moba Language (Togo), brought to completion by the friars of Dapango and printed in Paris. The other, the Bible in Chinese, is a monumental work, the first translation according to the original texts and the first popular edition. This was a task of seven Franciscan friars of the Biblical Center in Hong Kong, four Chinese, a German, a Frenchman, and an Italian who worked together for twenty-three years, completing it on February 6, 1969. The correction of the proofs itself took an entire year, and the proof-reading of more than three million characters.

Among the numerous enterprises of the Capuchins, one of the most successful was their work in Ethiopia, besides their beautiful traditional work in the Indies, the Central African Republic, Chad, Djibouti, Turkey, and Syria. The Ethiopian mission had the good fortune to be directed by three outstanding missionaries in succession: Bishop Massaia, OFMCap., beginning in 1853, then Bishop Taurin, OFMCap., and finally from 1900 to 1937 by Bishop Jarousseau, OFMCap., who knew the country and its inhabitants very well. Another flourishing mission at the present time is that of Araucanie (Chili) in the care of the Bavarian Capuchins, numbering 327,000 Catholics among its 345,000 inhabitants. In South America the friars of the Third Order Regular are quite active also.

The Order has been present in Morocco since the 13th century. For several centuries the various Christian communities (merchants, but also captives and mercenary soldiers of the army of the Sultan) had Franciscans as their chaplains. From the beginning of the 20th century, Franciscans were often the military chaplains. The presence of the sons of Saint Francis is at the present quite reduced but still active. The Franciscan Missionaries of Mary are spread throughout the whole kingdom. Many of the laity are active in helping to bring a Christian presence to a Moslem country and are often referred to as "cooperants," and their presence is referred to as "à la Franciscaine," conforming to Chapter XVI of the Rule of 1221. Charles de Foucauld and Louis Massignon began some of these efforts and worked along the lines of bringing the laity into missionary work.

Considering new missions, besides Togo, of which we have already spoken, new efforts have also been undertaken in Zaire; and after two centuries of interruption, the Franciscans returned to Japan where they became prefects apostolic of Sapporo and Kagoshima. More recently, the friars have undertaken missionary work in Abidjan, Madagascar, and Formosa.

In the last decade, the minister general of the Order, John Vaughn, an American, has requested that the Order give priority to the mission in Africa. He has launched an international missionary effort, the Africa Project, for which he solicited and obtained, despite the present lack of vocations, an international recruitment. As Saint Francis wished in the thirteenth century, the Order has placed itself at the service of the gospel in all of the world.

The Eighth Centenary

Nineteen eighty-two was a remarkable year for Franciscanism as the twentieth century draws to a close. The Order and the Church celebrated the eighth centenary of the birth of Saint Francis. This was a remarkable occasion for the renewal of research and creativity in all areas, but this time in the exciting atmosphere and aftermath of the Second

Vatican Council. Colloquia were organized throughout the world and remarkable expositions were held in many places. In the ampitheatre of the Old Sorbonne at Paris, conferences were held and the talks put together in a special edition of the *Review of the History of the Church in France*. Franciscans everywhere used the occasion to bring Saint Francis before the public.

Another manifestation of the vitality of the Order and the post Vatican Council atmosphere was the desire to return to the sources: the diffusion of the primitive documents of the Order, whether through the bilingual edition of the *Writings* of Saint Francis and Saint Clare, in the collection *Christian Sources,* or through the reedition of two volumes of the *Documents* (primitive lives and writings). Some of these had already appeared in partial editions, but were now collected, clarified, and made more easily accessible to those who were interested. The phenomenon of publishing was truly international. The French effort spurred the Spanish to come out with their edition. The Italians and the Americans followed their example, and now almost anyone interested in Saint Francis is familiar with the large red book known as the *Omnibus of Sources*. During the seventies in preparation for the centenary, and through the eighties these early lives and documents of the beginnings of the Order were published in each of the major languages.

One of the best results of the eighth centenary was the tightening of the bonds of fraternity among all the branches of the Order plus a recovery of and joy in a universal fraternity, an ideal that had always been hoped for but now began to exist in reality. Who knows if the blessings are not going to continue and make themselves felt in recruitment for all the branches of the Order where, at least after several decades of decline, there appears to be the beginning of a resurgence. As of January 1, 1988, there were 18,890 Friars Minor, 11,483 Capuchins, and 3,958 Conventuals, with 20,000

Poor Clares and 861 members of the Third Order Regular of men.

But statistics which can reveal many things, often hide essentials. What numbers are not able to tell is the interior renewal which takes place despite the aging of some communities; and this is as true for the Poor Clares as it is for the Secular Franciscans and even for the First Order.

The Second Order

Between the First and Second Order, structural and governmental differences are rather important. The deep bond which unites them is not seen by the superficial observer. Indeed, while the friars are an Order both public and itinerant, the Clares are cloistered nuns. The First Order lives a life that is called "mixed," where both prayer and action go hand-in-hand, the Second Order is composed of contemplatives. The First Order groups its friaries into provinces and possesses a heirarchic structure, while the Second Order is made up of autonomous monasteries. It is necessary to look beyond these differences.

One of the essential points common to the two orders which is demanded by the rule is the gospel lived in fraternity—it is fraternal life. Clare borrowed, moreover, from Francis a key idea that she simply changed to fit the feminine circumstances, "If a mother cherishes and nourishes her daughter in the flesh, how much more must each one cherish and nourish her sister in the Spirit."

What actually do the Poor Clares live on? Very often just the alms that are received. The custom is still kept, for example, of coming to pray in Poor Clare chapels and of placing, on the "turnstile" of the monastery, things bought at the market. These are called the gifts of nature for the "gruel of St. Clare." A dozen eggs is the most common gift, because people know that in the houses of the Poor Clares there is perpetual abstinence. But we live no longer in a totally Christian civilization nor in an agricultural society. In the twentieth century, the cloistered contemplatives also support themselves by making things, such as hosts or vestments, or of making other things needed in the liturgy and in the churches. A variety of works such as ceramics, paintings, sewing and knitting, or fulfilling some other local need are performed to enable them to live a simple life.

Today, a young woman who wishes to become a Poor Clare must have good health, although there do exist several communities for the sick who are dedicated to the imitation of the Crucified Christ. The young woman must have sure judgement and a right intention since one does not enter the cloister for negative reasons; she must also have proper psychological balance and a certain maturity. In the majority of cases the young woman is asked to give proof of this before entering the monstery by pursuing her education and earning her living for a few years before devoting herself to the cloistered life.

"The vocation of the Poor Clares, in the interior of the Franciscan family," writes one of the Poor Clares, "is a rooted vocation. What that means is burial and silence, but also a power of life and fecundity. A monastery of cloistered religious women evokes a well of living water which one can draw out endlessly. Like all the places on the earth where the tenderness of God flows, one finds here joy in the freedom of adoration and of the gift. Love joins in God all peoples and poverty becomes richness because a treasure has been discovered."

The Third Order

Renewal is also taking place in the Third Order or the

Secular Franciscans. One of the major facts in the present history of the Church is the awakening of the laity, a laity which discovers its own proper task and which assures it a more active and more conscious role in the Church each day. This post-Conciliar phenomenon is particularly concretized in the growth of the groups of the evangelical life which revolve in orbit around the great religious orders, and in stressing once again the binomial quality of life: action and spirituality. To the number of these groups of the evangelical life, the Franciscan Third Order, now called the Secular Franciscans, is attempting to rekindle its spirit and the dynamism of its beginnings when groups of people were running after Francis. It attempts to conserve the evangelical spirit but rejuvenates and adapts its structures to the conditions and needs of life in the twentieth century.

Pope Pius XII addressing himself to the Secular Franciscans of Italy on the first of July, 1956, said to them: "The spirituality of a saint is nothing other than his special manner of representing God, of speaking about him, of going to him, of treating with him . . . There is a Franciscan manner of contemplating Jesus, of loving him, of imitating him. The world has need of this Franciscan spirit, of this Franciscan vision of life. It is you who must know it deeply, to love it with enthusiasm, and to live it, and spread it."

Despite all the insufficiencies and the difficulties of the Order and of the individuals of which it is composed, Franciscanism is a current of spirituality which continues to attract and to retain, even in the twentieth century, numerous souls in search of an ideal. The radiant influence of the gospel as well as that of St. Francis is still attractive. With Francis one feels at ease with the Divine while at the same time perceiving the bracing demands of an incessant call to do better and to do more. The case of Simone Weil is not unique: never had she prayed, until in Assisi in 1937, at the Chapel of the Portiuncola, protected within the great Basilica of Our Lady of the Angels, something stronger than herself, she says, forced her for the first time to fall on her knees.

* * * * * *

This brings to a conclusion our rapid overview of the history of the Order. For the most part, we have stressed people and institutions, and perhaps that is rather a bit dry. Francis, the poet, also benefitted from the affectionate attention of artists and poets through the ages. Even before Dante had dedicated to Saint Francis a song in *Il Paradiso*, Henri D'Avranches had composed in his honor an epic poem of 2,600 Latin hexameters—and that in 1229, only three years after the death of Saint Francis.

It would take volumes to list all the authors and poets who have praised the Poverello through these seven and a half centuries. What a long list and what a variety of talents is represented in those who have spoken about him or sung his praises! It is truly the "Franciscan flood" of which Father Ubald d'Alençon spoke in 1926.

All these efforts are "a concert of praise most legiti-mate and justified," wrote Pius XI in 1926. "Again, it would be necessary," added the pope, "that Saint Francis provoke our imitation much more than our admiration. Because the Herald of the Great King had for his goal to lead all people to sanctity and not first by making them tender and compassionate friends of the flowers, of the sheep, of fish, and of birds." And Pope John Paul II, when he visited Assisi, summed up the heartfelt prayer of all people in these words: "I come as a pilgrim to Assisi, to the feet of Saint Francis, the Poverello, who wrote Christ's gospel in such incisive characters in the hearts of the people of his own times. The pope comes to visit this city, which is always a witness to that marvellous divine adventure which took place here toward the end of the twelfth century and the beginning of the thirteenth. It is a witness to that surprising holiness that passed over here like a great breath of the Spirit. A breath in which Saint Francis of Assisi participated as well as his spiritual sister Saint Clare and so many other saints born from their evangelical spirituality . . . . You who brought Christ so close to the people of your age, help us to bring Christ to our age, to our difficult and critical times. Help us! These times are waiting for Christ with great anxiety, although many of our age are not aware of it. We are approaching the year 2000. Will these not be times which will prepare us for a rebirth of Christ, for a new coming? Help us, Saint Francis of Assisi, to bring Christ closer to the Church and the world of today. Help us to solve everything in an evangelical key, so that Christ himself may be the Way, the Truth, and the Life for modern men and women."

An American poet, Vachel Lindsay, inscribed a poem that expresses our wish in these last years of the twentieth century.

> Would that I might wake Saint Francis in you all,
> Brother of birds and trees,
> God's Troubadour,
> Blinded with weeping for the sad and the poor:
> Our wealth undone, all strict Franciscan men,
> Come, let us chant the canticle again
> of mother earth and the enduring sun.
> God make each soul
> The lowly leper's slave:
> God make us saints, and brave.

SELECT BIBLIOGRAPHY

Original Sources and Lives of Saint Francis

Habig, Marion, OFM, <u>The Omnibus of Sources</u>. Franciscan Herald Press, 1973

Bodo, Murray, OFM, <u>Francis: The Journey and the Dream</u>. St. Anthony Messenger Press, 1972

Caretto, Carlo, <u>I, Francis</u>. Orbis Books, 1982

Chesterton, G. K., <u>Saint Francis of Assisi</u>. Image Books, 1957

Englebert, Omer, <u>Saint Francis of Assisi</u>. Servant Books, 1979

Fortini, Arnaldo, <u>Francis of Assisi</u>. Crossroads, 1981

Green, Julien, <u>God's Fool: The Life and Times of Francis of Assisi</u>. Harper and Row, 1985

Jorgensen, Johannes, <u>Saint Francis of Assisi</u>. Image Books, 1955

Manselli, Raoul, <u>Saint Francis of Assisi</u>. Franciscan Herald Press, 1988

HISTORY OF THE ORDER

deBeer, Francis, <u>We Saw Brother Francis</u>,
Franciscan Herald Press, 1983

DesBonnets, Theophile, <u>From Intuition to
Institution</u>, Franciscan Herald Press, 1988

Esser, Cajetan, <u>The Origins of the Franciscan
Order</u>, Franciscan Herald Press, 1970

Iriarte, Lazaro de Aspurz, <u>A History of the
Franciscan Orders</u>. Franciscan Herald Press,
1983

Moorman, J.R.H., <u>A History of the Franciscan
Order</u>. Franciscan Herald Press, 1968 (Re-
print, 1988)

Nimmo, Duncan, <u>Reform and Division in the
Franciscan Order, 1226-1538</u>. Capuchin
Historical Institute, 1987